D0188004

PRAISE FOR *Spiri*

A *Library Journal* 2020 Title to Watch

A *Remezcla* Book by Latino and Latin American Authors to Add to Your Reading List This Year

A *Book Riot* Must-Read Book Every Runner Should Read

"Alvarez's decision to discover his roots and learn how he could make a difference in issues that mattered took real courage. It was a resolution that passes from his mind to his feet as he pushes through thirst, hunger, animal encounters, hostile townspeople, and disputes among exhausted running mates. Through participating in Ceremonial Circles, he becomes part of each culture he journeys through, of each landscape he explores." —LAURA CLARK, American Trail Running Association

"Not only is it a striking story about coming of age and reconciling identity and history, but also about immigration and capitalism and how these are tied to labor and the land in inextricable ways. Is it also a story about long-distance running in a variety of landscapes? Sure. But it's also about a hell of a lot more, too." —JAIME HERNDON, *Book Riot*, 1 of 9 of the Best Nonfiction Books About Nature and Climate Change

"This memoir tells the incredible story of a young working-class man in agricultural Washington state who achieves a full-ride scholarship to a prestigious private school and gives it up to join indigenous runners on a trek from Alaska to Argentina . . . Álvarez's writing is vibrant and immediate." —WENDY J. FOX, *BuzzFeed*

"[Álvarez's] memoir *Spirit Run* recounts how a grueling ultramarathon offered a powerful spiritual reckoning with his ancestors, the land and himself . . . A beautiful amalgamation of Álvarez's part in the PDJ run from the brutal toll it took on his knees, the bonds he forged with other runners (and the arguments that arose), his run-in with a mountain lion—all while harkening back to poignant passages of his parents' migration story, with thematic connections to the run's ever-shifting spiritual focus." —KATHERINE OUELLETTE, *The ARTery*, WBUR

"Álvarez's story is awe-inspiring and full of wisdom about how to live with integrity, compassion, and love." —REBECCA HUSSEY, *Book Riot*

"Emotional . . . The book chronicles not only that epic run in 2004 but also the background of the author and his immigrant parents."
—RICH TENORIO, *The Guardian*

"Lyrical . . . *Spirit Run: A 6,000-Mile Marathon Through North America's Stolen Land*—part travelogue, part traditional memoir—comes face to face with the many strands of [Álvarez's] inheritance, revisiting Carver territory while treading a new path . . . The story of the striving, first-generation kid made good is a familiar one; Álvarez makes his ache." —DANIELLE JACKSON, *The New York Times Book Review*

"[*Spirit Run* is] more than another tale of blistered feet and dehydration. It's about the immigrant experience, about the indigenous experience—and finding one's place as a witness when you're neither."
—MARY ELIZABETH WILLIAMS, *Salon*

"Álvarez explores his Indigenous Mexican identity through acts of endurance, survival, and self-discovery . . . Running is an act of prayer that transcends gender, race, and nationality."

—MATTHEW SAKIESTEWA GILBERT, *Sierra*

"A gift for the reader." —LINDA BROWN, *Yakima Herald-Republic*

"A gorgeous rendering of both the physical challenges involved in running 6,000 miles as well as the different kinds of landscapes Álvarez and the PDJ crew traversed." —ALEJANDRA OLIVA, *Remezcla*

"This awe-inspiring debut memoir traverses 6,000 miles and is peopled by the unforgettable cast of characters." —KATIE YEE, *Literary Hub*, 1 of 10 New Books to Add to Your TBR Pile

"A remarkable account of a 6,000-mile ultramarathon relay through North America." —MOLLY MIRHASHEM, *Outside*

"Like the act of running, and like Álvarez's PDJ experience, *Spirit Run* is a complex, thought-provoking journey shot through with flashes of glory and hope." —KATIE NOAH GIBSON, *Shelf Awareness* (starred review)

"Álvarez maps not only the land but his own body; his own relationship to people, earth, and ancestry; and the perils of capitalist frameworks that shape our lives on this land. *Spirit Run* is a running book, a social and environmental justice book, an anti-capitalist book, and an epic journey book." —*Book Marks*

"*Spirit Run* is an eloquently written memoir by a young man straddling the world of his Mexican immigrant parents in the migrant-worker community of Yakima, Washington, and the mainstream society that beckons after he receives a full-ride scholarship to college . . . A powerful American coming-of-age story about a Mexican American who seeks to embrace his heritage while forging his own path forward. Certain to make a lasting impression on readers across generations and backgrounds, all of whom will be inspired by the young Álvarez."

—*Booklist* (starred review)

"The story of Mexican American Álvarez will speak directly to teens forging their way in the adult world."

—*Booklist* (YA) (starred review)

"Yakima native Álvarez debuts with a spellbinding narrative of his coming to terms with his place in America today . . . In electric prose, Álvarez writes of returning home and forging a new connection with the land and its communities . . . This literary tour de force beautifully combines outdoor adventure with a sharp take on immigration."

—*Publishers Weekly* (starred review)

"When the son of two Mexican immigrants hears about the Peace and Dignity Journeys—'epic marathons meant to renew cultural connections across North America'—he's compelled enough to drop out of college and sign up for one. *Spirit Run* is Noé Álvarez's account of the four months he spends trekking from Canada to Guatemala alongside Native Americans representing nine tribes, all of whom are seeking brighter futures through running, self-exploration, and renewed relationships with the land they've traversed."

—BECKY WADE, *Runner's World*,
One of the New Running Books of the Year

"A swift-moving lope across the continent . . . A thoughtful first book that should inspire others to lace up their running shoes and get moving."
—*Kirkus Reviews*

" 'I know now that every bit of earth contains the sacredness of another person's existence,' says Noé Álvarez in this riveting debut memoir, which ruminates on the relationship of the body to the landscape and what it means to call a place home. This account of a run is also a journey into the mind that, after incredible tests of endurance and faith, blurs the distinction between running and prayer. *Spirit Run* offers a distinct vision of the risks we must take to attain a life worth living."

—MARCELO HERNANDEZ CASTILLO,
author of *Children of the Land*

"Like all the best running books, *Spirit Run* is about much more than clocking up the miles. Álvarez's journey honors the migration story of his parents and the arduous crossings made by so many other Americans. *Spirit Run* is a stunning memoir that moves to the rhythm of feet, labor, and the many landscapes of the Americas."

—CATRIONA MENZIES-PIKE,
author of *The Long Run*

"Noé Álvarez's words beat with the pulse of our hemisphere. Through them, we encounter Mexican, Indigenous, and migrant stories that are distinctly, defiantly American. *Spirit Run* is an anthem to the landscape that holds our identities and traumas, and its profound power to heal them."

—FRANCISCO CANTÚ,
author of *The Line Becomes a River*

"*Spirit Run* is a remarkable book. In gentle, minimalist, profound prose, Noé Álvarez writes about his once-undocumented parents before going on to run thousands of miles with Indigenous people. He finds his own magic."

—DOUGLAS WHYNOTT,
author of *The Sugar Season*

"*Spirit Run* is the story of what brown bodies must do to reclaim identity and dignity. In language that puts us not only in the shoes but in the skin of the displaced, Álvarez takes back Raymond Carver country and tells an electric, kinetic, modern working-class story. So few books make me sweat and cry. *Spirit Run* has summoned breath and energy out of me."

—CINELLE BARNES,
author of *Monsoon Mansion* and *Malaya*

"This book is not like any other out there. You will see this country in a fresh way, and you might see aspects of your own soul. A beautiful run."

—LUÍS ALBERTO URREA,
author of *The House of Broken Angels*

Álvarez, Noé,
Spirit run : a 6,000-mile
marathon through North America
[2020]
33305255141081
ca 03/14/23

SPIRIT RUN

A 6,000-Mile Marathon Through North America's Stolen Land

+ + +

Noé Álvarez

This book is a memoir. It reflects the author's recollections of experiences over time. Some names and identifying details have been changed to protect the privacy of individuals.

Copyright © 2020 by Noé Álvarez

All rights reserved

Hardcover ISBN: 978-1-948226-46-2
Paperback ISBN: 978-1-64622-053-3

Cover design by Nicole Caputo
Book design by Wah-Ming Chang

Library of Congress Control Number: 2019944451

Printed in the United States of America
1 3 5 7 9 10 8 6 4 2

To my Mia, mother and father, brother and sister,
and all the working-class warriors hammering out
a future for the rest of us

Contents

Outline of the Run

British Columbia, Canada: Prince George, Alkali Lake, Lillooet, Melvin Creek, Mount Currie, Whistler, Vancouver.

Washington, United States: La Conner, Coupeville, Port Angeles, Neah Bay, Rialto Beach, La Push, Quinault.

Oregon: Portland, Eugene, Reedsport, Coos Bay, Battle Rock, Gold Beach.

California: Blue Creek, Klamath River, Weed, Mount Shasta, Redding, Covelo, Ya-Ka-Ama Forestville, Richmond, Berkeley, Oakland, Mission San José (Fremont), Watsonville, Santa Maria, Solvang, Santa Barbara, Montecito, Oxnard, Santa Paula, Piru, Pasadena, East Los Angeles, Anaheim, Chicano Park San Diego.

Arizona: Yuma, Ajo, Tucson, Nogales.

Mexico: Magdalena de Kino, Hermosillo, Bahía Kino, Punta Chueca, Isla Tiburón, Pótam, Ciudad Obregón, San Miguel Zapotitlán, Los Mochis, Culiacán, Mazatlán, Chametla, Acaponeta, Huajicori, Tepic, Ixtlán del Río, Magdalena (Jalisco), Teuchitlán, Guadalajara, Tonalá, Chapala, Ajijic, Tuxcueca, Sahuayo, Jiquilpan, Morelia, Pátzcuaro, Teotihuacán, Amatlán de Quetzalcóatl, Cuernavaca, Taxco, Ixcateopan de Cuauhtémoc, Oaxaca, Tuxtla Gutiérrez, Caracol Oventic, Acteal, Toniná, Cascadas de Agua Azul, Comitán.

Guatemala: Huehuetenango, Zaculeu Ruins.

Prologue

2003. Among the pines of Bella Coola, in Canada's British Columbia, Canadian authorities escort a seventeen-year-old mother, in handcuffs, to identify and unearth the site where she buried a baby son a few days earlier. The teenage mother's name—Crow, of the Secwépemc Nation, whose full name translates to "Water Waves"—is reflected in her tears. The baby she buried was her firstborn son, pronounced dead at seven weeks old. For forty-nine days her baby lived with the power of a name, under the protection of Secwépemc tradition of caring for one's own, blanketed with the dreams of a mother who sang to him until the very end, when he stopped eating. Fearing that the hospital would take him away, Crow wrapped him into his cradleboard and escaped with him into the forest.

She remembers that night in the mountains as very cold. The rain pelleted her as she and two others encircled the boy in a wall of ceremony before digging up a spot in the muddy earth with a shovel. The Secwépemc people bury their own. But on this February day the authorities unearth the body of the infant, Nupika Amak ("One Who Can Travel Between Two Worlds"), reversing the sacred order by which a Secwépemc mother makes peace with the loss of a son. They desecrate the earth in front of her—land that had laid claim to Nupika Amak's spirit—and bring him back to this world to be processed, tagged, and issued both a birth and death certificate. Then, they take his mother back into custody for questioning.

When asked why she didn't register her baby: Because she wanted him to be a freedom baby. Free from government oppression.

✦

In 2004, in a salmon fish hatchery in Chickaloon Village, Alaska, where snow is still thickly packed onto the ground, and the air cuts a person's face like obsidian glass, thirty-year-old Chula Pepper, a traveler from San Diego, California, stares into a mirror of a bathroom with a Swiss Army knife in hand. No job, no relationship, no home. She grabs her long hair and cuts, like sickle to wheat, long, black strands, before settling onto the cold floor. Nearly bald. She shivers over the few things to her name: a backpack, some clothing, a sleeping bag, rain pants, and a troubled past. Tomorrow, she decides, life will be different.

✦

In the small town of Smithers, Canada, nineteen-year-old Zyanya Lonewolf of the Gitxsan and Dakelh Nations quits her job flipping burgers at a McDonald's and relinquishes her role as caretaker of a household in torment—an incarcerated father, a drug-addicted mother, and a murdered cousin along Canada's Highway of Tears. Against her mother's wishes, she withdraws what little savings she has from an ATM, purchases a backpack, and breaks from all she has ever known to join a caravan of Indigenous runners.

✦

Still farther north, in one of the coldest parts of the Vashraii Koo, or Arctic Village, Alaska, an elder named Ipana packs her life of sixty years into five oversize suitcases and travels to join the others—Indigenous runners from across the world congregating in Alaska for a race through North America toward Panama. In Fairbanks, Ipana, a leader in the Dené territories, a community aligned with the migration patterns of the Porcupine caribou, faces a wind and thinks about those ancient runners who had passed through these lands, migratory protectors of the sun who had moved with the herds of caribou.

The time has come for Ipana to find within herself the spirit of those runners, the Sun People, to find the courage to leave home and spread an urgent message—the Arctic is dying.

✦

Around the same time, in Oakland, California, twenty-nine-year-old Cheeto awakes to the day on which his dream will come true. A dream of a run that unifies all the people of the world and that takes him far away from an area he no longer feels a part of, the Bay Area, to which he was brought over from Mexico when he was only two years old.

He has quit his job at EB Games, said goodbye to his nieces and nephews, and scavenged the Bay Area's thrift stores for warm clothing. He packs his backpack, takes farewell photos with family, then washes down a couple of Heinekens at a going-away party this afternoon. The next morning he boards a gray van, which will take him to Alaska.

✦

Alone in the Haslett Basin, in the foothills of the Sierra Mountains in Fresno, California, a man dials into his Apache and Purépecha heritage, beating a drum for guidance. Here, beside a fire pit among ponderosa pines, in ceremonial sweat, Andrec prepares himself spiritually and mentally to colead runners through North America. He meditates for the courage and the clarity to lead Indigenous warriors safely across vast lands. He sings and stokes the fire, calling on the wisdom of his Apache mother and Vietnam-veteran elders who taught him about committing to things that are bigger and greater than oneself. He channels the wisdom of the medicine bag around his neck—"Apache protection," he calls it—and drives a gray van all the way down to Los Angeles to pick up runners, before driving far north to Alaska, in search of that person that his father wasn't.

✦

In Arizona there's a man whose soul is branded by the tragedy of the copper mine strike of 1983. He, Pacquiao, the main leader of the run, was about ten years old when he witnessed his hometown of Ajo, Arizona, on lockdown, martial law enforced, the town besieged by bulldozers, snipers, police, and the National Guard. It was an event that displaced many residents, separated families, and converted the place into a near ghost town.

For four days and four nights Pacquiao—of Yaqui, Tohono O'odham, and Ópata heritage—submerges himself in ceremony in an arid region of southern Arizona. He sweats, fasts, and prepares himself to carry forward the immense weight laid upon him two years prior by the elder Gustavo—his mentor, a prominent labor-movement leader, and the founder of the sacred ultramarathons across North and South America, held every four years, known as the Peace and Dignity Journeys. Pacquiao co-organizes, with Andrec and Chula Pepper, a safe route across North America, starting in Alaska.

After securing and loading up the vans, Pacquiao leads a caravan north to Chickaloon, Alaska. On the way, he gives lectures and picks up runners.

✦

In Sonora, Mexico, two Yoreme Nation brothers—Mazat, also called "*El Que Corriendo, Mata,*" or "He Who Runs, Conquers," and his older brother Greñas—take leave of their families and university studies to hitchhike several days north to the U.S. border. They journey to fulfill an obligation to their elders: to surrender to the run and embrace the way of the warrior—those committed to the protection and preservation of the land, animals, and their people's culture.

✦

These are only some of the marathoners of Peace and Dignity Journey 2004. They are ordinary people proud of their heritage, summoned by a call greater than themselves.

✦

And then there's me.

Spirit Run

WE

I

Warehouse White Noise

Even the sun yields to the massive gray structures dominating the small town of Selah, Washington. They are fruit production and distribution centers—*empaques* as they're called in Spanish—that confine migrant labor inside, as prisons might. Here, apples, cherries, and pears are packaged for delivery across the globe.

These warehouses stand only five minutes from my house in Yakima. Here, and throughout the rest of the Yakima Valley, men with guns—hired policemen—idle at the front gates of the private property. At shift change, security personnel in reflective vests direct the flow of employee traffic by flagging figure eights in the air like on airport tarmacs. Day and night, semitrucks bearing hillocks of apples grumble in and out of the premises. Towers of apple bins—twenty-five-foot beacons branded with the company logo—stand in the sun waiting to be loaded. They slice shade from the unrelenting heat and, each day, a little bit of dignity from the backs of the laborers. This shade sundials onto the blistered hoods of cars that Mexican migrants carpool inside of in 110-degree weather. Boys, almost men, operate beeping forklifts, hauling fruit cargo in haste. Parched winds whip against a limp U.S. flag the size of a large billboard, as if to remind us whose land this really is. Summer heat waves lean into the backs of working men, women, and minors like me, employed for the summer—sixteen-, seventeen-year-olds—as they exit the sauna of packed cars and swarm the fruit-packing warehouse for a chance at a meager paycheck.

At shift change, the people in their company lime-green shirts burst out of the warehouses. Among them is my mother, Carmen, whom I accompany for the first time the summer of 2002. I'm seventeen, a junior in high school, and in this part of the country, kids much younger than me are expected to work. Some drop out of school to support their families. This summer my mom and I work the day shift together, although she usually works nights. When people scurry past me, I look into the harried faces of the working class, my people, Mexicans and non-Mexicans. We are united and divided by our condition. There's nothing uplifting about this kind of work. I look at myself and my green shirt. I'm not any different. To be young and in high school means nothing to a place like this. Soon, I fear, it will consume and trap me like all the rest, my dreams of ever leaving Yakima ending here.

My mother's identity, in her decades working here, seems to have been reduced to a company shirt that clings to her skin in dark shades of sweat. ID badges hang around our necks. A pass to work—to exist. We hurry inside, where deafening generators run and metallic sounds reverberate, throbbing in our heads long after shift has ended. The place is a confusion to me, a complex mess of man and machinery designed only for one thing: to package fruit. The by-product: the erosion of the minds of the people working here. We walk through an invisible wall of icy air that sends chilly beads of sweat down our bodies. My mother pinches her shirt and fans it in the cool air, but the cold quickly consumes her in a shiver and she puts on her sweater. We split off, men and women to separate quarters of the building. Like sleepwalkers, people take their stations. Gray walls and blinding commercial lights around us direct people's gazes downward. My mother, a sorter, slouches over one of the many conveyor belts of fruit, shoulder to shoulder with other women, in a valley of mothers, grandmothers, and even great-grandmothers all conditioned to believe that this is all they can do with their lives. Little by little the company has stripped them of the things that identify them as individuals. They have removed their watches and jewelry. Their hair is tucked beneath blue hairnets. They do this until their individuality is largely erased. They become one monotonous shape, the shape of a worker. The conveyor belt flows with apples, pears, and cherries, depending on the season. Delicate fingers sort the fruit picked by the hands of mothers who live all across the Yakima Valley, fruit that ends up in stores, farmers' markets, and ultimately in homes across the globe.

The bosses are stationed above us, in mezzanine offices. They are vigilant. Some prowl the scaffolding with clipboards and walkie-talkies. A few senior-status Latinos are charged with supervising us, wearing a false sense of belonging and authority as though it were a badge. They pit us against one another, then reward us with company swag and lunch boxes.

Many times this summer I observe my mother hard at work. Harder than any mother should be. I watch her going through the motions, planted among machines. Nothing I can do about it but hold out for the day I will graduate from high school and go off to college, become a small-town hero, return a different man.

Until then, my jaws clench at the thought that my mother's body is being molded by the demands of apple-orchard owners. Her feet, shoulders, and hands seek relief from her sinking, stiff posture, her aches and misaligned joints. Blood queues in her calves in the form of varicose veins, and she shrugs at the pinch above her shoulders where the muscle has thickened like a bull's hump. A similar deformation is taking shape in her knees. Only now, this summer, do I learn the pangs resulting from standing for long hours in a factory. The uncirculated blood below the knees crushes my feet. I wonder how my mother has sustained this for as long as she has. Decades. I feel sorry for ever having been impatient with her, for not being more helpful around the house, and for not fully understanding what the warehouses were doing to her mental health. Years of toiling in these conditions has left her too beaten down to start anew.

I now begin to understand why my mother didn't want me looking for a job here. She was probably afraid of what I'd see or, worse, that I might view her differently.

But despite her misgivings, as soon as I was old enough, strong enough, I insisted on working with her at the factory. I am hoping to alleviate some of the financial pressure. Hoping, in my own naïve way, that I can do something to save our family, the unit that is clearly coming apart at the seams. What I am learning is that we aren't making it as a family. I blame Yakima for stretching us too thin. For keeping us separated on holidays and weekends because bills needed to be paid and food needed to be bought. For years I avoided facing this, knowing that I might crumble beneath the weight. To delve into this misery was not helpful to surviving the years. But my parents have lost the spark between them. Love for them has become just another part-time job on top of two or three other jobs. The thing about love is that it doesn't put food on the table. Working alongside my mother forces me to open my eyes. College will protect me. I have to save up enough money, somehow.

I think of the moments when my mother called me at home after school during her lunch breaks. There's food in the fridge, she would say. Not just the beans and rice we ate almost every day, or the tortillas lathered with butter and salt then scrunched into balls. Special meals that she cooked at night, at the end of her shifts, while I slept.

When I can, I wave to my mother on my way to an even colder section of the building, inside the freezer, where the product goes for storage. Even I can't escape the mark of labor tainting my shirt, soul, and mind. I'm demoralized by the images of my people almost prostrating before machines. I despise the way it touches me. The touch of toil. My eye sockets sink with exhaustion, fruit stains my clothes. My lower back aches and my feet feel hammered with nails. There are days that I can't help but feel a certain shame when looking into my mother's eyes. And it is for this reason that I hate the warehouses the most.

I begin to doubt if I can ever free my mother from the assault of the fruit industry. The harder I work, the more I feed into the whole enterprise, the more tired I get of fighting, the more I hate who I become, and the more I become part of the problem—I become efficient at the thing that I don't want to become efficient at. The harder I work, the more I begin to believe that I am only useful for my physical strength. I bottle up the worry for a later day, daydreaming about college counselors, financial aid, and course catalogs—when my time will come to do greater things far outside of town. I have to get into college. I have my high school counselors for guidance. I can pester them for information on colleges, financial aid, and tell them that the army is not for me—as is expected. Many here join the army in hopes of winning their citizenship.

"Amá," I call out to her on my way to the bathroom where long lines force me to hold it in. My voice can't shake her from the rapid river of apples. "Amá!" I shout against the clicks and clangs of metal mouths hounding my mother.

What chokes me up is the sight of her hand, hiding from the prickles of tendonitis and tucked between her left breast and soft stomach. Her hand is tender within a wrist brace. It brings her no comfort. Her other hand does the work of two, grabbing at the fruit as best as she can. Once again I shout to grab her attention until she finally forces a smile at me.

My mother likes to talk me up to her friends. They look at me like someone who could help change things around here. Here is as far as they go.

✦

The alarms sound. The machines convulse again with rage for man and woman. Unforgiving. The speed increases. The shouting from above resumes. My mother's eyes fall over the belt again. I enter through plastic doors into another massive wing where fruit is stacked and stored. The temperature drops by several degrees. The roar of forklifts is in my ears as I dart through the mayhem to my spot at the end of "the line." There, the conveyor belt unleashes its tantrum of large fruit boxes. Diesel clouds from the forklifts act upon my nose like smelling salts and give me a jolt of energy that I take out in anger on my work. This is for my mother, this is for my father, this is for all the working-class people—of all races and colors, who have to put up with living like this.

My gloves tear at the fingertips, nicked by the rough handling of boxes, and I suck my cuticles clean of blood. The taste of machinery is inside of me now, the iron taste of blood. Extra gloves come out of our paychecks so we keep quiet.

I'm on stacking duty, or *estaquiando* as the men call it. The men no longer look me up and down like they did the first day, as if to say, "He won't last," "Quit wasting my time," and "Here's another young sucker, fallen like the rest of us." Maybe now they see me as part of their own, something I both want and don't because it means that I'm adjusting. But I hate that success means that I must see myself as something "better," as non-Mexican. Maybe if I could keep seeing myself as something else, as something "better," I'd help end the vicious cycle of hard labor. But this is a privilege many people here don't have. They can't afford to see themselves as better than their condition. At least not yet.

The men and I wait at the end of the line. Our teeth chatter with cold like Morse code, secret messages decipherable only by those living inside. Hands rest on hips or under the warmth of armpits, chests expand rapidly after a flash of work, and eyes remain tunnel-visioned to one task: readying ourselves for the next batch of boxes. We say little during the calm. Our faces glisten with sweat. After each man readies his pallet behind him, he waits for the new barrage of product. It's during these moments that I become acquainted with a new kind of cold: warehouse cold. It's a cold that seals lips, that seeps into bones, that presses underpaid workers to work like robots. Our bodies chase after boxes for brief embraces of warmth. We put on flannel coats but still shiver. We pat our arms and stomp the cold from our feet like men caught in a blizzard. Regularly the memory of what goes on inside and outside these walls beats inside of me, while the other men and I march in place for warmth. Outside, somewhere on an orchard or construction site, my father continues to pick fruit or hammer nails into buildings that will stand long after him. I conjure the good hours, when I'm not at work, when I am among other Latinos who sit on their lawns BBQing carne asadas, sipping beer, listening to music, happy that another day has been endured.

We stand along the belt, muscles cramping from constant hot-to-cold transitions. The bellow of generators and machinery blends all noise together into one cacophonous hum. The warehouse white noise.

The buzzer sounds. Like clockwork, we pivot our weight, moving rapidly, tapping into our reserves to pick off fifteen-pound boxes like butter from the conveyor belt, stacking them onto blue wooden pallets. We hunch low over these pallets, gradually stacking them as we build them so high that we have to stand on our toes. Nine boxes per level, fifteen levels tall. We lift boxes with all our strength onto the pallets towering well above our heads, pushing with our shoulders and then fingertips. The product rises and rises, labels facing out. The labels must always face out. When they don't, pallets have to be disassembled. I'm still getting the hang of it. Pallets must stand straight. When the pallets get too tall, I learn by watching the other men how to flip boxes into the air like pizza dough, but with the weight of fruit. I feel something like pride when I catch on. A glimpse of joy, even, at the thought of beating the machines. I'm glad to be of help and ease the load of my coworkers. At the very least, I'm not a burden to them. But the joy is short-lived. Our hard work is used against us. The machines are recalibrated to move even faster.

There are two conveyor belts in my section of the warehouse. When one of the two lines queues up with too many boxes, everyone kicks into high gear to help. Boxes swell and slam into one another, piling up and knocking onto the ground. Someone will get fired for this. The boss can't allow for damaged fruit. One after another, boxes pile up while we struggle to rectify the collision. Men from other lines dart over to assist us, while also attending to their own line. Young and old men race back and forth between the lines, working with all their might to beat the indomitable machine. Sometimes this chaos brings a smile to someone who then yells a sort of war cry, known to Mexicans as an *aipa*. A sort of, "Bring it on, I'm strong enough!" It lightens the mood. It inspires me to do the same and work in harmony with my coworkers. But the smile soon leaves my face when we lose out against the apple apparatus.

This thing, this life cannot be beat.

If the line proves too overwhelming, a supervisor pushes the emergency button, stopping the conveyor belt. He waits until all the boxes are cleared. We, the defeated men, are reminded again that we are only men. Nothing more. Less, even, in the face of all this metal. White and Latino supervisors scold us for the delay, and before long, the buzzer sounds again, giving us little time to recover. Several times a day, for long hours, this is the routine. It's difficult to think clearly. The common response to the question of what time shift ends is, "When the trucks stop coming."

✦

I must imagine my people as they really are. Not as I want them to be. Maybe then things will change. Maybe then it will hurt me enough to work harder to improve their conditions.

✦

My shadow drags behind me as I step outside momentarily for lunch, into the blinding sunlight, and sit, pounded with exhaustion. My aching body does weird things in the transition from the cold warehouse to desert heat, similar to when you put frozen hands into hot water. My body swells and tightens against my skin. My rose-tipped nose and fingers burn with thawing and I scrunch my face to regain feeling there. My cold ears pop and for a minute I cup them with my palms to ease the sharp feeling. I sit on the sidewalk against the tall cement slabs to eat my food alone. Tacos de frijoles. Too tired to speak or chew. Workers everywhere crowd outside under the shades of hedges, or sit on old picnic tables, or lie down on the freshly cut grass in front of the management office. Do they not see us?

I look to my mother gesturing animatedly with one hand on the far side of the cafeteria among girlfriends, walking back inside with her lunch box. It's the end of her break. I see now that here are where all her friends are. She has built a life here. Her family outside of family and the reason she will probably never leave this place. Breaking ahead is a lonely venture without one's people.

✦

At the end of our long shift several hours later, my mother and I exit the icy cavern. My body thaws again in the hot weather. The warm air outside smells of hay. It's evening and I swell into my clothes. I can barely make a fist with my hands. We walk to the car among the streams of other men, women, and old acquaintances of mine who should have gone back to school the year before but didn't. They lie to teachers and tell them they're returning to Mexico when, in fact, they use the time to work. No one at school checks. People cram into their cars to drive to other jobs in orchards, at warehouses, and on construction sites. What they make here is not enough to live on. The new arrivals walk inside for evening and grave shifts. Day and night the fruit river runs. I drive the car past the front gates and the stationed police car while my mother closes her eyes in the passenger seat. We drive into the silent landscape where the ringing in my ears catches up to me. Not very many cars drive these roads. The sky is clear. I sink into the warmth of the car's seat and resist dozing. These roads are occasionally used as checkpoints by the authorities. ICE in this desert landscape. It's a part of small-town policing, in which officers seem eager for the next warehouse raid—but only after people have done a full day's work, and only near the end of the harvest. My mother's lunch bag rests on her lap. A bag of apples sits at her feet.

The landscape is gorgeous. Along the horizon, ancient rock structures, basalt ridges tower over these lands. How much more beautiful everything would be without all the warehouses obstructing this beauty, without racial tensions dividing people. We hit a small bump in the road and it half wakes my mother. She takes a moment to remove her wrist brace and massage the swelling. "We're almost home," I tell her. She dozes off again. I look at her wrist, at the large knob keeping blood from her thumb, and I can't help but think that one day her hand will fall off. Company doctors tell her she's in perfect health, to quit complaining, and that she can continue to work. Whatever the company needs. When we get home she goes straight to her bedroom.

✦

The next day I knock on her door at one in the afternoon. No answer. I then try the doorknob. It's unlocked this time. The door is obstructed by boxes and it opens only an inch. The lights have been on all night as usual. I press my face against the sliver of the doorframe and peek in. My mother is curled up under her thick Mexican blankets.

"*Amá. Desayunamos?*" Breakfast time.

The human lump underneath the nest of blankets sighs. There's not much space to walk inside her room. Towering shoe boxes, black garbage bags, and laundry baskets filled with neatly folded clothes flank her bed on three sides. Her vanity is plastered with photos of Catholic saints and of her sisters in Mexico. There's a picture of me, slouched and posing with my peach-fuzzed face, and of my siblings. There are *pomada* ointments and cure-all creams everywhere. Dust coats everything. Why she surrounds herself in so many things, only she knows. But it looks as if she's ready to run away, ready to run back to her sisters in Mexico.

"*Amá. Ya son la una.*" She sleeps too much these days. But no amount of sleep can bring her body peace, it seems. I close the door slowly, walk back to the kitchen, and cover the plate of food I prepared for her. Everywhere in the house are bags of rotting apples: on the kitchen counters, dining table, in cabinets, and on the floor. There are probably more apples in the trunk of my mother's car. No one in the house eats them anymore. But no matter how much this family has outgrown their taste for apples, I know that my mother will continue to bring them home. It will take me many years to understand why. I go through these bags of apples remembering that for many years they were what helped feed us when food was low. One by one, I toss them into the trash, feeling as if I'm throwing my own mother aside. They are her source of pride. For me, they are everything evil. Hidden beneath the sweetness of every apple, under the unblemished rinds and the MADE IN WASHINGTON labels, are the face and touch of someone's mother.

When she wakes in a sort of limbo state, she turns on the TV to her Spanish soap operas. My father is still away at work. "*Mijo. Dame masaje, sí?*" She falls into the sofa, her muscles aching. She kicks her feet up, closes her eyes, and I put my hands over her forehead.

Like kneading hard clay back together, I press my fingers as hard as I can into her scalp and work-hacked muscles. I imagine reconstructing her flesh and rebuilding her lost youth with the tips of my fingers. It's like massaging concrete. She tells me that her hurt does lessen. "*Gracias, mijito.*"

I shovel my mom's Mexican pomada cream onto my palms and press underneath the arches of her small feet. They're like rocks. Her calluses feel like sandpaper. I press her arches with my knuckles, trying to work my hands into the pressure points of her superhuman feet, and then trace the streams of her protruding varicose veins back into her calves. They disappear, but only for a second.

I shake out the cramps in my hands before moving to her tough hands. They're dry around the cuticles from her constant hand-washing. Whatever it is, it cannot be washed away. Her palms are tough like lizard skin. Wrinkled and sinuous. Her nail polish is chipped. When I massage over the bruise-colored knot in her wrist, she jerks her hand back as if bitten by a snake. These are the hands of the woman who has endured a journey across Mexico and who made a life for me in the U.S.—the first and only woman in her family to leave Mexico. This woman whose thumb now hides and adheres her index finger like a splint, a casualty of migrant life. She falls back to sleep and I pick up her small shoes and wrist brace and curse that cold place where we work. I put the television on mute and look into her face for a moment, recording the moment, thinking about that inevitable day when she will no longer be here, no longer suffer in a town that made her pay for being Mexican. I press my lips against her forehead and walk away.

2

The "Palm Springs of Washington"

When the rhythms of working-class life cut inside me like broken beer glass, I run. I run in order to dislodge my problems from where they have taken up residence, and I come upon the Naches River with my parents' stories in hand. I run hard until my thighs burn, toward the tributary of the Yakima River, until I can finally clear my throat of anger, slapping my face and chest to remind myself of this heavy flesh—the burden of being human.

I run to find relief and to help activate a power within me, pushing myself hard over hot pavement as if to extinguish flames from my feet. To find courage along a river that flows beside mobile-home parks, graffitied landmarks, beer-hops factories, and gravel pits. The river and I run next to the Boise Cascade lumber mill, with its stacks of felled logs.

We run by a billboard that reads WELCOME TO YAKIMA: THE PALM SPRINGS OF WASHINGTON, a name intent on covering up the messier realities of the town.

Here, east of the Cascade Mountains in Washington State, where the sun shines roughly three hundred days a year, is my desert, my hometown of Yakima. The summer evening air swells to the high nineties. Hay mounds, truck stops, and cattle dot the landscape. A sun-baked barn is painted with the words GOD BLESS AMERICA. In this region, rich volcanic soils, turned over by the hands of many generations of laborers—beginning with the Yakama First Nations People, then people from Europe, Africa, Japan, the Philippines, and now Mexico—have made this land one of the world's leading producers of apples, hops, cherries, and wine grapes. It is a paradise on the surface, but its history is harsh. It is a region that cycles through its most vulnerable people—immigrants who plant and plow.

Someday my parents too will pass into the volcanic soil that enriches the region and that I now caress within the palm of my hand along the river where I pause to catch my breath. When I resume running, I kick my feet into the ground and huff between my steps, moving into the peripheries of the camps of homeless men and women who live in tents along the river, among the tall brush, littered with beer cans and syringes.

This is Raymond Carver country—an area whose working-class narratives have been articulated to the world in the short stories of the local author.

Here, along the rivers, old hills, and ghettos, I do most of my thinking about what it means to be a son of immigrants, what it means to be working-class, and what it means to run and explore the land on my own terms. To find forgiveness on a land that feels, sometimes, like it has broken me. To carve my way out of Carver country and create a new path for myself.

3

Ganas in Carver Country

Cruising is another way high school youth like me examine our future. Tonight, the cockpit of my friend Chilo's car—a 1981 Chevy El Camino, nicknamed "the Hawk"—smells of engine oil and orchards. Rigo and I sit while Chilo jams a screwdriver for a key into the ignition. Now that our summer jobs at the fruit-packing plants are behind us, and college applications are submitted, we make hanging out really count. The Hawk's engine starts and its chassis shudders. This is our last summer together. Chilo's mom, born in Jalisco, Mexico, who cans fruit at the Del Monte factory, calls out to us, "*No anden muy tarde.*" Chilo nods, hooks his arm over the door—an arm tattooed with the 509 area code—and reverses from the driveway. A rosary undulates from the rearview mirror and he drives toward Fourth Avenue to a stop sign that's edited in blue spray paint. Local gangs with a message for those who will listen.

Here, in this northeast part of town, where desert wildflowers consume rusted cars, rose bushes flourish near cornstalks, and broken glass from car thefts riddle the streets like mosaics, immigrants and working-class families live precariously, working hazardous jobs on uncertain legal statuses, doing their best to keep their teenagers safe from gang violence. Still, families push forward. They tend their many clucking chickens and jalapeño gardens; they hold barbecues, and play Mexican music, lending a hand, hammer, or wrench to anyone in need. Even the children, shirts tucked and sweeping sidewalks or mowing lawns, put in the work for their people—the balm that soothes suffering.

Even with the Hawk's windows rolled down, beads of sweat roll down my face and I lick salt from my upper lips. A hot gust enters the car and blows Chilo's hat hair from his eyes, styled from the orchards working alongside his father.

They keep me strong, give me hope, friends whom I met sophomore year of high school, when I joined their ranks in honors classes, sitting quietly in the back of the rooms. As solitary and quiet as the Yakima-bred Raymond Carver who attended this school in the 1950s. A working-class boy like us who went on to become one of the greatest short-story writers of all time—a writer who captured the extraordinariness of ordinary people and their reckless acts.

Within a one-mile radius of our school, you can find three gas stations, a rundown bowling alley, an overcrowded mental-health clinic, and a jail. In the distance, the green Del

Monte water tower pokes its head above the town, stalking us. The train tracks that demarcate the town into East and West are no longer representative of the division between poor and rich neighborhoods—only poor and slightly less poor. The rich have flocked to the hills above us and into orchards on the West Side.

We still seem trapped in the cycles of Carver's narratives, as if his words condemned us to a world of loneliness, tarnished relationships, and violence. Seen differently, his words urge youth like us to rewrite ourselves out of these sinkholes.

To sprint out of them.

✦

Tonight, my friends and I gather at the Fruitvale Trailer Inn where one of the Farias brothers, Miguel, has lent us his home for poker night. Buy-in: twenty-five cents. No one knows it at the time, but for nineteen years, he will live under constant police surveillance as an undocumented person. He will be deported several times and he will one day be placed in solitary confinement at the Tacoma Detention Center, three hours away from Yakima, and remain in custody there for fourteen months. He will participate in a hunger strike against the poor conditions there. He will, eventually, miss his father's funeral.

This night, his eyes droop, perhaps with exhaustion. His is a face thickened by work in the outdoors. "Here are the keys," he says, soft-spoken. "Lock up when you guys are done." He gets into his truck and leaves for work.

The three of us and Miguel's younger brother sit on the front steps of the trailer under a dull bulb, clinking Smirnoffs. Moths flutter, crickets sing, and a Confederate flag hangs from a neighboring trailer. Inside, on a table, is a scattered deck of Mexican cards and the trace of young men trying to make sense of life over a game of conquian and music because it's hard to put into words that which is better conveyed with the gestures of camaraderie. "*Camaradas,*" we say. Still, every day I try gathering words as our people do apples, ones to help keep me moving forward. Words that help me imagine what I struggle to imagine in this town.

That I am worth something.

"One day, I'm buying those houses," I promise, speaking of the million-dollar ones, "all of 'em." I point toward the hills on the West Side of town on Scenic Drive and beyond, where the tall mansions try blocking out the horizon. But the hills and the people below them know better. We do not wish to be cast under a shadow. That's why some of us say we'd rather level them to let the land breathe. Or, like me, to, "Buy them all up and give them away to the poor."

On a night like tonight I look at my hands as if that's all it takes—physical strength—to make everything right, succeed.

"One day I'll buy the orchard where my dad works. We'll work there, but as owners," Chilo promises in the light tic of his tongue. "We'll call it the Casteñeda Orchard," he says, after his family's name. His view of the orchards and life in general has always been more positive than ours. That always centered me. It was he, in fact, who'd introduced me to the works of Carver.

We create pacts over french fries and tacos, and stack onto our shoulders the kinds of promises that weigh on first-generation youth: to be the ones who save our families from things like poverty, deportation, and harsh labor conditions.

✦

Back in the Hawk, I think back to the year 1995, when I was ten years old, working in the fields alongside my father throughout the year, and during summers and weekends:

✦

One day, I was under a tree deep in the center of an apple orchard, when I lifted my face from the blanket, startled by the movement of animal life around me. Hints of tractor diesel pinched my nose in the crisp air of *la mañanita*. As usual, dew drops dangled from the tips of grass blades. Branches arched low with the weight of apples, crowding out the horizon.

Sitting up, cold and stiff from the lumpy earth, I inhaled the sweet smell of apples decomposing on the ground around me in brown rot. Birds reeled in worms like spaghetti, while squirrels trapezed between trees that trembled from my father's plucking hands. His torso was deep inside the ball of foliage and his legs stuck out against the rungs of the tripod ladder. His boots squeaked against the ladder as he climbed down with a picking bag attached to his chest. He leaned over one of the wooden bins and unloaded the bag of fruit, then stripped it from his chest and dropped it onto the grass. He polished two apples against his faded blue pants, before resting against the base of a tree next to me.

"*Ten, cómete esto.*" He handed me an apple before spitting pulp into his own hand and tossing it to the birds. Long hat hair escaped from under his trucker hat and over his ears. The inside of the hat was imprinted with my father's sweat, that distinctive head smell.

For a while we sat, absorbed in the soft sounds around us. My father sipped at his thermos before finally speaking.

"*Mijo,*" he paused. "Never be like me. Like any of this," he said. "Get out when you can." He then picked up his bag, collapsed the fifteen-foot ladder over his right shoulder, and slipped away into the tunnel of tall grass and apple trees.

After a while, I hung my blanket over a branch and hurried to help my father in his work.

✦

Work was my initiation into manhood. The way into my father's love. But it wasn't always fun. I tended to the vegetable garden, carving into the crusted earth with an old hand plow, clearing the area of weeds and maintaining the perfect ripples my father had already drawn into the land. The hot summer sunlight wrung salt from my sweat into my eyes. My palms burned with blisters.

As a child, it was a need of mine to explore, lured everywhere by animals that I'd give chase to far into the outer reaches of the orchard. Once, at the edge of a DO NOT TRESPASS sign posted on a barbed-wire fence, beyond the faint outlines of migrant housing—a cinderblock shack with a tin roof, and beyond-corroded smudge pots that stood erect like cigarette butts in an overcrowded ashtray—I stumbled upon the fetid remains of a coyote carcass ensnared at the paw by a metal trap. Its mouth was agape with maggots and flies, as if frozen in a moment of agony. These were the darker sides of orchard life. Shotgun shells riddled the banks of a slime-green pond where swallows dove after their own reflections one inch from the water's surface, whisking off a top layer of bugs. Chattering finches rendezvoused in the spiny blackberry bushes. Big-bellied robins in orange puff ties stood at attention while squirrels scaled down trees headfirst.

But work came first. In addition to working on the orchard, I fed chickens and collected eggs from the tarp-and-wire aviaries my father built.

✦

I pushed myself to work hard like my father, pushing hard against rest.

In the evenings, when the air finally cooled and the sun was nearly receded behind the hills, we jumped into my father's truck, the bed sinking with the weight of his tools. I observed if my nails were as black with dirt as his as we reversed out from the orchards as men.

✦

As soon as I was old enough, I awoke from the delusion that nature was good to my people. With time I became suspicious of orchard and warehouse life. By the time I reached the age of ten I had already been well acquainted with my social class, with working with my hands and imitating my father in the apprenticeship of hard labor. I learned that I was poor, monolingual, and from a struggling family living the sort of day-by-day life that had no clear end in sight. Only apples and more apples. I saw my own reflection in my father's fears.

On the orchard, everything seemed to sweat no matter what time of the year—the trees, the grasses, and our bodies. Farm bugs, ticks, and mosquitoes pestered my ankles and wrists while I worked. I pulled weeds that lacerated my palms. Dust collected on my face, neck, and nostrils. Even in the winters I sweated, and my knuckles bled in the dry and frigid air.

I was born into the life of dirt. My hands inherited the marks of the Latino farm laborer.

On this unrelenting land, in a small plot, I helped

cultivate cabbage, chard, zucchini, green beans, and asparagus for the owners. I dragged five-gallon buckets of water and birdseed to caged chickens, pheasants, roaming peacocks, and other game birds.

In many ways I wanted to be like my father because of his superstrength. Work brought me closer to him. I wanted his long hair, his calloused hands, and even his afflictions. When not tending to the birds, or picking apples from beneath the trees, I raced to relieve my father from work. "I can do it," I'd tell him. He was always on the go racing like a man who was still homeless and hungry on the streets of Mexico.

He taught me how to see. With the heart of my hands.

✦

For hours, Chilo, Rigo, and I sit like this in the car, dreaming that Yakima will change, that it will accept us with open arms, and renounce its assault on migrants and poor, working-class people. This is how we soak in the timeless evenings. We talk about who we'll take to prom, summer jobs in the orchards with our fathers, or sorting fruit in warehouses with our mothers. We don't talk about the things that really bring us down: friends' suicides and murders, the drug overdoses, juvi incarcerations, or the Middle East—where Chilo's and Rigo's brothers will deploy to, one of them hoping to win his citizenship by enlisting.

4

Getting Out

One day my senior year of high school, catching my breath from a long run home, I check the mailbox and see a package. Taped to it is the long-awaited letter from Whitman College. All the other schools to which I applied wait-listed or rejected me. Whitman, my last hope, will undoubtedly also reject me. On the front steps of my house, I brace myself in private for disappointment.

I consider tearing up the letter. I do not want my mother, who is inside the house, to share in my defeat when I open the letter. I can tell by the smell emanating from the front spring door of my house that my mother, who always insists on expressing her love through food, is preparing my favorite dish of enchiladas. "*Vas a desaparecer,*" she'd often jest about my weight.

"Congratulations!" the letter announces. In a mixed moment of joy and anger I slam the package as hard as I can onto the front lawn, forgetting myself. I feel so much joy, and anger for all the times I was told to set my goals lower. Anger for all the times that I was reprimanded in elementary school for speaking Spanish, and the times I was made to do janitorial community service because, as people said to me then, "that's what Mexicans do." Cleaning other people's messes.

I open the box and run inside with a big smile, to show my mom its contents. My mother, who embraces me in excitement, loosens her grip around my waist when she realizes the significance of the letter that I translate for her. To her, leaving home is like leaving the country. People who left Mexico, like her, never returned. If they did, it was only after many years had passed. "But look, Amá," I say. I try to reassure her that times are different, that I will visit her. And, I show her, "The college sent us onions." She inspects the Walla Walla sweet onions silently, places them on the counter, and turns to the boiling pot of chicken. Things will be different now, I try to convince myself. I fold the letter, put it in my back pocket, wash my hands, and help her dice some college onions, feeling conflicted.

Later, my father walks in through the back door and removes his heavy boots. His eyes are red from a long day at work.

"*Apá,*" I call out as he sinks into his chair at the dining table. The same table he'd regularly have me sit at when he needed me to translate papers, to read to him in Spanish, or simply someone to unload on about his time growing up in Mexico. Mexico, where he survived his brother's murder, and his mother's fatal car accident. Where he survived a father who abandoned him, and survived living in hog pens among rats. The many times he dodged starvation. Now, my father eats from the plate my mother has set in front of him quietly, pinching tortillas into his mouth.

"Apá, I have good news," I say.

His face is still stuck in the shock of somewhere else. He never seems happy and I usually give him his space. He's happy about the college letter. I leave it there. I don't tell him where I'm going to get the money to pay for school. That would be a conversation for another day. I let him rest.

✦

A couple of months later, my family accepts an invitation to attend the Hispanic Academic Achievers Program (HAAP) banquet—an event held every year at the convention center in Yakima honoring college-admitted migrant students and presenting them with scholarships. I am happy that I am being considered for a scholarship, but we are not told in advance how much support we will receive. Still, I see my parents in a new space, polished, and that means something. My mother has treated herself to a new dress and a visit to a hair salon. My father bought the works: a clip-on tie, a dress shirt and pants that are a little baggy, Payless shoes, and suspenders that don't quite match the rest of his outfit. Their rough hands rest on the soft white tablecloths.

A mariachi band plays in the background. Steaming hot plates of Mexican American food are served to Mexican mothers who make comments about the rice. Too much cumin. Their home-cooked tortillas are much better. Eyes glance around for direction on how to proceed, what silverware to use first, and some jest about what items to steal at the end of the banquet. Some brought Tupperware.

Finally, students line up onstage. Rigo and Chilo go up to the podium before me. When my parents and I are finally called up to the stage, my heart beats as hard as that time when in middle school a car full of bullies tried running a friend and me down through alleyways and backstreets. The ceremony isn't over, and already I am afraid of being run down in college by the pressure to do great things. To secure the career that will solve all my problems.

Then, the host announces: I have been awarded a full ride. I shout in excitement and punch my fist into the air. I look over at my parents, their faces aglow with pride as we shake hands with the governor. Finally, at least for today, I bring them happiness. My mother grips her arms tightly around my waist. We can't believe it.

I will finally get out of town.

5

Walla Walla Walkabouts

On a bright weekend in August 2003, I move to college. Whitman College is in the small town of Walla Walla, three hours southeast from Yakima. My family and I make a road trip of it. We traverse the desert towns of Toppenish, Wapato, Sunnyside, and the Tri-Cities along vacant highways. My parents have traveled these lands for work before, and occasionally we have visited relatives, but this is different. A son off to college, a journey steeped with meaning and pride. My father's eyes are fixed forward, his thoughts projecting onto the fallow lands. What lessons will he have for me now?

The car's radio signal cuts in and out between the valleys. We often keep it tuned into Radio KDNA, "the voice of the *campesino*," the nation's first full-time Spanish-language radio station. It has been known to alert immigrants of immigration roadblocks and ICE raids by playing songs with themes about *la migra*. To my right, the loyal Yakima River runs alongside our car. I imagine myself alongside it again, running the Yakima Greenway trail one last time before it veers off into the distance for good.

✦

After a long trip, we exit the CITY CENTER ramp in Walla Walla—"the land of many rivers"—into the bubble known as Whitman College—the school of notable alumni like actor Adam West and former Supreme Court Justice William O. Douglas. The school's mascot at the time is "the Missionaries"—people who brought destruction upon the Natives. A historic 1920s building, the Marcus Whitman Hotel, towers high over the silent town.

"*Que bonita tu escuela*," my mother comments about the campus.

Seen from our passing car are shirtless, long-haired hippies in harnesses rappelling the rock-climbing walls of the athletic center. Girls in bikinis dip inside a large fountain near a stately all-women's residence hall and sorority. The brick facade of Prentiss Hall overlooks Lakum Duckum—a geothermal spring that keeps ducks around all winter long. Trimmed hedges and rose bushes carve out a path toward a creek and tennis courts. The watchtower of the admissions office, green with vines, casts its elegant shadow over the twenty-four-hour library—one of the few in the country and already in full use by students.

We look on, our faces softened by the shock of so much paradise.

We get out of the car and step onto this new ground gently, as if expecting it to crumble beneath our feet. My father comprehends the wealth and intellectual power around us, and for the first time, I see fear on his face. I look around, waiting for someone to approach me, to tell us that we're at the wrong place, and that it's all been a mistake. But no one does. The paper in my pocket assures me that Lyman House will be my new living space. We creep toward the dorm, thinking that there's a secret etiquette to everything here. We get what feels like sympathetic looks. On a field nearby, people play the unfamiliar sport of lacrosse—a game I would later learn has its origins in Native American culture. Everyone but us seems to be perfectly in their element.

We enter my white-walled two-room suite on the third floor, where we're welcomed by my Hawaiian roommate and his father. They gift us with leis and chocolate macadamia nuts. In return, my mother nudges me to hand them a bag of apples. I'm embarrassed that these overripe fruit are a reflection of me. I unload two duffle bags onto my bed, open my window, and stick my head out. Barefoot jugglers and tight-ropers gather below on the grass. In that moment I am overcome with a wave of optimism and think of all the things I will accomplish in college. I will study politics, change the world through social activism, and make money to help my family. The smell of my mother's food fills the room—tacos tied in grocery bags warming my new desk.

"*Tienes que comer bien.*" Eat well, my mother says.

"*Te va ir bien. Te va ir bien,*" my father repeats to me. "It'll go well," but really he says it as if to himself.

✦

Later that day, after my parents have left, I brave the dining hall for the first time. The buffet lines are full of confident eaters who seem to have arrived knowing what to do. They seem like connoisseurs of food culture and taste as I watch them serve themselves delicate portions, their plates colorful with evenly balanced food groups. I look nervously at the nutritional details and descriptions of foods I've never seen, smelled, or tasted before. Words like, *vegan, toxins, paleo, organic, grass-fed,* and *soy-based* don't help clarify for me what the foods actually are. I notice some people glancing at me and my confused plate—a mess of different diets: tofu on top of ground beef on top of tempeh and cheese. With two mounds of food finally gathered onto two plates, I stand scanning the intimate tables for people who look more like me. There's witty, comedic, rapid-fire exchanges among people who appear to understand one another's ways. People crosshatch around me. Hardly a person of color to be seen. It is one of the many spaces where I have a lot of catching up to do. A place where people knife and fork their pizza slices and dab napkins over the edges of their mouths. The kind of place where no one slurps bowls of soup or eats with their hands. Tortillas are something else in college. They're burrito wraps and not finger food. I can't eat normally here. Out of nervousness, I take multiple laps around the buffet stations, buying time, collecting myself while I read and study my environment—rehearsing in my mind for that moment when I will summon up the courage to squeeze myself at a table between friendly strangers.

On the following nights, I sit in my room, my stomach growling, staring at my clock and waiting for that crucial fifteen-minute window before closing time to enter the dining halls to eat alone.

✦

College is a difficult transition. I scramble out of bed, dash late to classes, fall behind on my readings, and process lectures and conversations in a mental fog. It takes its toll. Whenever I talk to my family on the phone, I feign happiness. "*No te preocupes, Amá,*" I say. I try to reassure my mother that I've made many friends, that I fit into the culture just fine, that I'll graduate in no time, and that I will come home to her a better and stronger person. And of course, that I'm eating well.

"*No te quiero flaco, mijo.*" I don't want you skinny, she says.

My family does not know that I spend entire days hiding in my stuffy room, downwind of my roommate's humidifier, looking out of my window and punishing myself with impossible expectations and the pressure to make my family proud. To come up with smarter comments and questions in class. To act on campus in ways that don't out me as poor and ignorant. I conceal my sadness from my mother when we talk over the phone. On my desk are piles of homework and professors' notes requesting to discuss my substandard performance. I fear confronting the world outside my room, because it is so intent on reminding me how unprepared and unintelligent I am.

Ancient Philosophy is the one class where I find a needed groove. There I discover Socrates and Aristotle, under a professor who speaks passionately and fearlessly about things like happiness, violence, ethics, and, "The unexamined life is no life for a human being to live."

When I'm at my worst, I run into wheat fields, where my outline melts into the night. I never forget what my father said to me: "It's either college or the fields, Noé."

I have confused the negative Latino stereotypes for my own story, like an earwig burrowing into an ear, and internalized them for truth. I have second-guessed myself every step of the way, becoming ashamed of who I am and who my parents are.

Running helps vanquish these feelings. It reminds me that I have been telling myself the wrong story—that I don't really belong, that we Latinos are an inferior people, that I am incapable of mastering the English language and moving confidently through the English-speaking world. And as long as I keep repeating these stories to myself, I will never escape their realities. In order to become someone else—achieve the full potential of my being, I have to engage in new imaginative acts. Running is one such act for me, a bonding with the world through the soles of my feet.

This chance to live a different and meaningful life, to confront my fears, comes to me in April of 2004.

6

Cold Feet

In April 2004, I attend a student-activist conference two hours south of Whitman College, at Eastern Oregon University. Before a workshop on Native American spirituality, presented by Pacquiao, a brochure catches my eye, about a run through North America, it says. North America? That can't be right, I think to myself. The brochure announces a marathon of Indigenous runners that will commence in Alaska one month from now, in May, and finish at the Panama Canal six months later. I read more of the literature:

> Peace and Dignity Journeys occur every four years and start with Indigenous runners on opposite ends of the continents (Chickaloon, Alaska and Tierra del Fuego, Argentina). They run for six months through hundreds of Indigenous communities where they participate in

> their respective spiritual practices and traditions; spark dialogue on the issue of peace and dignity for Indigenous peoples; model their responsibility to Mother Earth, Father Sky, communities, and themselves; and receive the community's prayers. These prayers and conversations are then carried to proceeding communities until the runners reach the center of the hemisphere. When the runners meet at the Kuna Nation in Panama City, Panama, it will symbolize all Indigenous peoples joining together in a spiritual way to manifest the prophecy of the Eagle and Condor.

This was the year PDJ dedicated itself to the women. Four years before, it dedicated itself to the elders, and four years from now it will be for the seeds.

It hits me. This is what I want to do. My paternal grandfather, who I know only through my father's stories, is of Purépecha Indigenous descent in the southern mountains of Michoacán, Mexico. I roll the itinerary in my hand and sprint to the classroom where Pacquiao holds his lecture.

I arrive to his class and find a seat—low attendance—in time to watch a video of people in Aztec headdresses wafting people in copal smoke, playing rattles, flutes, singing, drumming, running, and I'm immediately drawn in.

"We're learning how to be human again," a deep voice narrates over the flash of images of Native American men, women, and children, running with feathered staffs in their hands through different landscapes and countries—through deserts, jungles, city streets, and remote villages. Their ankles rattle with shells while they dance and run.

In all my excitement, I'm transported to Toppenish, Washington—home of the Yakama Nation—and tucked twenty miles south of my home in an equally dilapidated, dust-washed setting, beside junkyard lots, downwind of chicken- and cattle-farm odors. It was there, as a young boy, in a town of roughly nine thousand people, that I first developed an interest in Native American culture. A place WHERE THE WEST STILL LIVES, according to the town's billboard. I have family there, which meant regular drives through the historic downtown where wooden saloon structures line the streets like the Wild West. Saloons depicting roughly seventy historical murals of Native Americans, bison, plains elk, gray wolves, and bighorn sheep that roamed the open plains. As a child, these images—the long-haired tribesmen racing spotted horses, the tipi encampments on the horizon, the majesty of wildlife, all called to me on a spiritual level that I didn't fully understand at the time. I looked to these paintings of the Yakama Nation for hints of some direction in my own life—people who, like me, lived on the peripheries of society.

Pacquiao explains what running means. "To our people, running is our connective tissue and a form of prayer. But it is not for everyone and the run will quickly teach you that." There are many obstacles to conquer, mountain slopes to overcome, emotions to rein in. The bad weather, physical pain, and living with scarce comforts. All in order to invoke the spirit inside of us in the ritual of running.

I learn that PDJ has its origins in the United Farm Workers of America's 1966 march from Delano to Sacramento, California, to protest the working conditions of Latino and Filipino grape workers. It was a strike that lasted five years.

"In 1966, the people marched with an image of something that resonated with them—the religious symbol of the Virgin Mary—and in a way, that is how we lead the PDJ run today," Pacquiao says—"under the symbol of the feathered staffs—symbols of a people's struggles. In the end, a march is about learning how to work with the staffs, what it means to carry something like that, the stories and prayers of people."

Running renews our responsibility to community, he says, our feet being like drums that "if listened to long enough, can alter the human heartbeat."

He tells us that the run, though led by Native American communities, is open to everyone willing to put in the work. It operates in relay form—two vehicles help drop off and pick up runners in intervals of at least ten miles a day. Runners then cycle through two, sometimes three or four drop-offs, or stretches of running, a day—depending on the destination. Meaning, runners often surpass the daily minimum-ten-mile-run requirement, running up to thirty miles.

"We need people who can run," he says. People who don't

mind running twenty or thirty miles a day every day for the next six months. People with a great deal of self-discipline. People who can survive on little food.

People in the audience look around at one another. This is crazy, we're all thinking. But, my heart can barely contain itself.

Orchard life has contaminated my relationship to the land. I saw the land assaulted with pesticides, uprooted with shovels and tractors, overharvested with apple trees, and bordered with animal traps. Animals caught in these traps were then dumped into a pond by the owner. I grew to hate the land for what was done to it, and for what it had done to my parents, whose calloused hands I can never forgive, nor forget.

Students start trickling out of the classroom while Pacquiao starts to pack his bag. In a few minutes Pacquiao will walk out of my life forever, and I wonder if I'll ever get another chance at something so majestic. There's no clear answer. But my life as it is offers me nothing better. College is not the answer. My parents' hearts will break if I do this, and that hurts me.

But on the run is where I need to be. Out there, fully immersed in a new kind of chaos, in the wild, alongside Native runners, and relearning to be myself. A place where I can learn to be a better and a stronger son to my parents, a journey where I can push myself to the limit and begin to approach the pain of migration. I want to honor my parents' journey to the United States by embarking on my own adventure, and run on my own terms.

✦

On a friend's suggestion, I walk to the office of the president at Whitman College, up the winding stairs where a nice receptionist escorts me through a set of large doors to greet a tall man in a white, long-sleeve shirt, and a great smile. My pitch: funding assistance for a one-way airplane ticket to Canada. I try to explain, but all I can manage is, "I need this." He takes one good look at me, turns to his desk, and writes me a check for $500.

"Now, are you sure that this is going to be enough for you?" he asks.

I assure him that it's plenty, thank him, and we shake hands.

✦

With only one month to get into physical shape and make arrangements, I purchase a one-way airfare to Canada, and I drop out of college. I keep the brochure close, to remind myself why I am doing this:

> In 1990, over 200 representatives of Native Nations throughout Turtle Island [South, Central, and North America] met in Quito, Ecuador, to discuss, strategize, and take action on issues affecting Indigenous People. Elders discussed the prophecy of the Eagle

and Condor. This prophecy to unite Native people supports the goal of all Indigenous People and Nations uniting after centuries of colonization.

Inspired by this prophecy, elders proposed Peace and Dignity Journeys as a way to realize this unification. Through spiritual running and networking, Indigenous Peoples as a united force, from all over Turtle Island, can reclaim peace and dignity by honoring Indigenous values, ways of life, and current struggles of resistance to modern civilization.

Peace and Dignity Journeys aim to organize spiritual runs to heal our Nations through prayer from the effects of colonization; honor our elders and traditional people; honor Indigenous children, womyn, and future generations; remember all of our ancestors; continue the struggle of those that resisted invasion and colonization before us; promote peace, justice, respect, and dignity between all people; honor the sacredness of Mother Earth; create vehicles for cultural exchange between Indigenous Nations in which art, dance, music, and ceremonies can be shared and respected; celebrate the strength, survival, and self-determination of Indigenous Peoples and our ability to preserve our languages, cultures, and spirituality for over 500 years. (Peace and Dignity Journeys 2004, Oakland, California)

On my nineteenth birthday, May 26, 2004, over dinner at the El Sombrero Mexican Restaurant in Walla Walla, I inform my parents of my decision to join the Peace and Dignity Journeys runners in Canada in three days' time, on May 29.

My father remains quiet, as if already having anticipated this moment many years prior—aware that we are not yet free of our family's restless conditions. Survival is what compels us to move. He eats quietly as I continue to explain to them the specifics of Peace and Dignity Journeys—only the parts that don't seem too scary. I don't tell them that I will live outdoors, that I don't intend on returning to school, or that I don't have much money. Instead, I tell them that I'm going on a little vacation, with friends. That I'll be housed in hotels and fed gourmet food. I don't tell them that I have no idea where I'll be, who the people I'm joining are, and that, in reality, I don't quite understand the logic of the run and that I'm scared shitless. My father can see through me, but says nothing. My mother scolds me for giving up college.

"*No quiero que te vayas, mijo,*" she argues.

We finish our meal in silence, and in three days' time, my father and little brother drive me to the Sea-Tac Airport in Seattle. It is my time to explore the world on my own.

RUN

7

The Arrival

I come to Prince George, British Columbia, Canada, by a small airplane that flies above green mountains so unlike the desert browns of my Yakima. It's the twenty-ninth of May, 2004, and it has already been one month since the runners departed Alaska on May 1. The small plane lands in an airport closest to the camp of runners.

Two women from the run, Ipana and Kara, greet me, and I follow them outside, one bag over my shoulder. I inhale this new air deeply. It's icier, crisper, almost sweeter than anything I have inhaled before. The surrounding mountains are massive and green.

"Thank you for coming for me," I say. "I was worried that no one would be here to pick me up. Pacquiao hadn't returned my calls."

They tell me that communication with the outside world

is difficult on the PDJ run, especially in the woods, where the runners have set up camp. Pacquiao—the only one equipped with any real technology, which is to say, a basic phone, camera, and laptop used strictly for his work—is often away from the camp coordinating with communities for supplies of food and accommodations for runners to sleep. His equipment is off-limits to runners.

"At first we didn't know if you were our guy. But then we knew," Ipana says, smiling from the passenger seat while Kara drives. The car rolls onto a gravel road and rocks over potholes that start to make me nauseated. I crack open the window for relief. The air is wrapped in an aroma of wildflowers and sap warming in the sun.

"How'd you all know?" I ask. "My gear?"

"Your shoes. Could see them a mile away." They laugh. My shoes are neon yellow. The brightest objects in this part of Canada.

In addition to those shoes, I have a change of clothes, a journal, and a 1,600-page dictionary that, I argued to myself when I packed, contained all the books in the world.

The camp smells of cedar smoke when I finally step out of the car and, with my shirt, wipe the light rain fogging my glasses.

Slouched and huddled around the thin coils of smoke rising from a dying campfire are people who look as if they've just come back from battle. They have a hard look on their faces, ones that weigh heavily from all the running—their spirits low from one month of intense marathoning. They're tired. Tired of eating and sleeping too little. The discomforts of the outdoors, and their wet, molding clothes. Tired of the daily adjustments, setting up and breaking down camps, runners bailing out on them, and tired of newbies like me coming and leaving, invading their space, eating up all their food, causing problems, proselytizing ideologies, and not pulling their weight.

Around them, garments hang from clotheslines between a trailer home and various trees. In the distance, the faint sounds of a radio playing rap music. I notice a jeep—Pacquiao's—and two vans—a large brown one and Andrec's gray minivan. A man wearing large headphones—Cheeto—is cleaning the inside of the vans, sweeping the upholstery, and tossing out trash bags.

Under the hood of the brown van is a former gangster by the name of Trigger, from East Los Angeles. He's wearing a tank top, has a shaven head like me, and has swirls of tattoos on his arms. He walks up to me, wringing a dirty rag with his oily hands.

"Can you run?" he asks, measuring me with his eyes.

"Well enough, I think," I say. I notice scars the size of bullets on his chest. Sundance ceremony scars.

His eyes stay with mine until I look down. "We'll see," he says, and walks back to the van, throwing a nod to one of the bigger guys sitting around the fire pit.

The others, continuing to cast suspicious eyes at me, smoke cigarettes around the fire pit. They stoke the embers and mumble things to one another without so much as a welcome. Behind them is a dome-shaped sauna that I later learn is used for ceremonial sweating—a sweat lodge.

"Nice shoes," a big guy named Tlaloc finally shouts. He's shirtless. He wears a red bandana around his neck, has long curly hair, and is dressed in military pants cut into shorts. He has a ripped physique like that of Rambo—a name he insists people call him. When he calls me by a derogatory nickname to refer to my weight, I don't answer. The stuff of bullies, I can already tell.

"Set your stuff down anywhere. Make yourself at home," Ipana tells me, before disappearing inside the trailer.

I look around for a place to pitch my tent.

"Not there," Tlaloc shouts again and approaches me, his curls hanging over his eyes. "There," Tlaloc points with his knife to some mounds of dirt, away from his own tent. It doesn't look right, but I know nothing of the forest or ant mounds, and I do as he says. Tlaloc disappears inside his green canvas tent. I realize that any one of these guys, who are tough as hell, can easily snap me in half and disappear me in the woods. No one would know where to find me, we're so deep in the forest.

I turn, looking for some sort of direction, trying to absorb the culture. I see the profile of another shirtless man bathing under a patch of sunlight. His name is Refugio, a Mexican living in Saskatchewan and now stretching and rubbing ointment on his legs and ripped calf muscles. He's in his fifties, but doesn't look it. His body is like jerky—tanned and chiseled like an action figure. Like a crown, he ties back his greasy black hair with a folded bandana containing the partial image of the Virgin Mary. The runners are a blend of cultures. The tattoo of a large sun encompassing the whole of his back is revealed when he goes to meditate beside a bundle of sticks. There are about a dozen or so of these staffs resting against the base of a tree. They are engraved, decorated with intricate beadwork, and sinewed with feathers. Refugio closes his eyes, cocks his head up toward the sky, and his face becomes taut with a grand smile, gracefully inside his own world of meditation.

Wanting to prove myself, I spend the remainder of the evening taking an ax to a felled log, helping cut wood for the sweat lodge.

Andrec walks out from behind the trailer with his head hung low, combing through the length of his long wet hair with his fingers, as if he just showered. It sways only inches above the ground. While braiding it tightly into one long strand that hangs to his knees when he stands erect, he studies me with sorry eyes almost. He walks off, hair whipping behind him like a lasso.

✦

When it begins to rain, men and women disappear inside the mouth of the sweat lodge—a structure braided in wood and enveloped in fur to contain the heat rising from hot rocks within, when water is poured onto them. It is a permanent structure, a sacred space that houses about eight to ten people.

Rattles and drums resonate from inside the lodge like a tremor in the earth. I crawl into my tent and into my sleeping bag, with a tremor of hunger in my stomach, waiting for tomorrow.

✦

The next morning, I wake up wet to the sound of a conch shell. When I stick my head out of my tent, I see that the runners are gathered in a circle around the staffs, staring back at me. Mine is the only tent still up.

"We leave in ten minutes," Pacquiao shouts as I hop out of my tent, and, nervous not to give myself away as a first-time camper, collapse it incorrectly.

When I join the circle of runners, I make another mistake.

"You have to enter the door on the north side, over there," Zyanya Lonewolf tells me with a kind voice. Ceremonies, she says, have spiritual doors. The door is invisible only to me. She is from the Gitxsan Nation, nineteen years old, like me, and this is also her first day on the run. We smile.

Cheeto pitches in, "You have to turn counterclockwise before entering. Then they'll smudge you, then you have to pick up one of those staffs over there. We run with staffs here." He's originally from the Mission District in San Francisco "back when it was real," he will tell me later.

While runners get smudged in sage smoke, Refugio picks up the main staff, called the Father Staff. It is the one that encapsulates the whole of all the other staffs and that leads the run every day. It can be carried only by those capable of running especially long miles. Those who can carry the spirit of the other runners forward. The responsibility is intimidating.

Everyone follows Refugio's lead. We select staffs one by one. Me, I pick up one at random, though it is supposed to be the one that calls to me, as Cheeto says. Mine has talons.

Some laugh and others sneer at me picking up a staff. These feathered sticks are representations of the specific communities that donated them, are supposed to aid us on our runs. Staffs have specific origins and stories, and I get the feeling that not everyone wants me handling them. Nothing about me says *Indigenous*. Ceremonies and everything about this run is new to me. I'll just have to prove to them, and myself, that I can run.

Pacquiao concludes the gathering, and the runners scramble to get ready to run with nothing on their person but their feathered sticks and what they can carry in their pockets, if anything. The vans are packed with food and water, donated and purchased with funds from PDJ and packed into boxes and coolers that runners sit on between rotations on the run.

He announces that the run will proceed into the towns of Lillooet, Mount Currie, and Melvin Creek.

Our last stop will be Alkali Lake, Pacquiao says, roughly 180 miles south of Prince George, B.C., Canada.

That will be our next camp, where we will sleep, then depart the following morning.

After Alkali Lake, the plan is to run through Mount Currie, Melvin Creek, Whistler, and into the city of Vancouver, roughly 350 miles south, before crossing into the U.S. and into my home state of Washington.

While everybody breaks up and jumps into the large van—to be dropped off in intervals of at least ten miles, to run alone—I run to the gray minivan where Andrec finishes cinching up everyone's belongings under a tarp atop the van. Stuck to the side of the van are the circular stickers of the PDJ logo—footprints over the colors red, yellow, white, and black. "Sorry, man," he says while standing on the roof of the van. "I gave everyone three calls, already. We're closed up until we reach our destination." No more room for today.

I drop my pack onto the ground.

"To all you new runners," Andrec announces to the group, "welcome to the longest prayer in the world."

The runners have crowded inside the vans among the coolers, canned food, and other supplies. The van sinks with their weights and odor. They don't let me on. They tell me that newbies run first and that those who don't wake up early enough run carrying their backpacks.

"But how am I supposed to run?" I say. No one has explained this to me.

They point me in the right direction and tell me to run straight. "Stay on the gravel road," someone yells. Only

Pacquiao, Andrec, and Chula Pepper navigate the maps and chart the courses.

Runners run mainly with luck on their hands.

They tell me the PDJ motto: "When in doubt, turn left." That way, if I get lost, I'll be running in circles and will be easier to find.

The van begins to creep away slowly across the camp, with everyone inside but me. I walk alongside it, asking, "How will I know when to stop running?" There's only one gravel road that I can see.

"When you see something that looks like it's not supposed to be there," someone says jokingly from inside the crowded van, and they all begin to laugh. That *something* will be my ten-mile marker—a pile of rocks, sticks, or a water bottle with a red ribbon tied to it, they tell me. Finally someone shows me a water bottle: "Look for this."

Tlaloc takes my bag and closes the door. "I'll make sure you get it at the end of the run," he says, pretends to search in the bag.

"There's a hardboiled egg left for you if you want it," Cheeto shouts from the back of the van as it slips into the mountains without me. I take a moment to tie my shoes, when rain begins to pelt me. I look around. Nothing in sight but pine trees. I look at the gravel road, which seems more of a trail. We're far from any city or major town. This is my shot. My first run on the Peace and Dignity Journeys.

I quickly pocket a hard-boiled egg from the picnic table and take off running after the van, thinking that if I run fast enough, I just might be able to keep pace with them and not get left behind, or maybe even tell the driver to take me back to the airport. But what would my family think of me?

I plunge into the forest a new man, stomping through puddles, breathing in the wild country air of these green mountains. When in doubt, turn left. Sons of bitches. Rain, sweat, and fear drip from my eyebrows, and I'm suddenly feeling like I've just been had. Scammed. All my stuff gone. I run harder, and now feel truly alone.

Water comes from above and below, my feet dropping into potholes and rivulets of rain streaming down my face. These shoes are light. And because they're light, their bottoms feel thin, and aren't as good for running in the outdoors over sharp rocks, gravel, and now mud. They will bruise my feet. My chest burns from swallowing sharp winds that bully me sideways. In all this excitement I forget to pace myself to conserve my strength. The forest is all about pacing, and I still have five months to go, having joined the runners one month late. In all my running along the Yakima River, I had never calculated my mileage. Running was never something to measure—it was always about burning through my emotional fatigue. I doubt I ever pushed myself past ten miles, let alone the fifteen I am now tasked with. I do what has helped me before in the fruit factories—breathing in beats, two in, two out, recalibrating my running form to the rhythm of my feet.

Running is rhythm, I remember Pacquiao saying.

After a long and laborious stretch alone along the gravel

road in the forest, I stop at a split in the road. I look around for that thing that shouldn't be there, a water bottle, a sign of some sort, as if I'm supposed to know the sorts of things that don't belong in forests.

In their early days in Yakima, my father and mother planted pine trees deep in the Cascade Mountains, bandaging the land after logging companies wounded it. After a long day's work, my parents gathered around a fire among other campesinos who lived like they did—one day at a time. They shared their food and what little they had with one another.

"We said little during those times," my father would say to me at the dinner table when he shared stories of his past. "That was the way of the campesino—concerned only with things like who's hiring next, the next job, location, pay. We really couldn't talk of our dreams or plan too far into the future."

Between the months of March and May, when seasonal work in the orchards was low and there were no jobs, immigrants flocked to the mountains in work vans and trucks.

"We worked two, three months in Naches, Tonasket, Wenatchee, Chelan, and all throughout the White Pass," my father told me. It was work that he did for a handful of years. "Those months were cold, wet. Sometimes there'd be snow and we slept cold."

They were sixteen years old, my mom and dad, knowing not a word of English as they labored in the mountains. They slept under tarps strung from cars, under the canopy of trees, or packed inside truck beds. They hadn't met each other at the time.

"The men operated machines," my mom told me. The machines were augers, used for boring holes in the ground. Behind the men, the women canvassed the forest carrying sacks of saplings, plugging the holes with life, with their hands and feet. They brought their own food and gear, which wasn't much. Some showered in the icy rivers, but most didn't. They labored in damp weather and crisp air, among the bears that watched them from a distance. But it wasn't the bears that my parents feared. It was hunger.

They worked in a cold that lingered in their bones and that nudged them to move like this Canadian land nudges me to run today. During lunch breaks they huddled like penguins around their food, shivering. They rubbed and patted themselves down for warmth to revive sensation within them. Only after a long day did they settle around a campfire, where the heat thawed their bodies and soothed them to sleep in their respective corners, wrapped in the scent of hard work.

✦

On the gravel road, small rocks and twigs piled into a pyramid formation instruct me to run left, to where Andrec is parked on the shoulder of this thick forest, waiting for me in the gray minivan and listening to Native American music. I jump into the van shaking, still catching my breath, and he drives me ahead, sixty or seventy miles or so, to where the runners are, and where he will drop me off again to repeat the run.

"Good. You're still with us," Andrec says, lowering the radio, while I take off my wet shoes. My toes are withered and whitened. Aching. Out the passenger window I peel my soft egg, then eat it.

Andrec turns on the heat for me. "There's a quicker way to peel those," he says. "I'll teach you later." The trick of blowing into the cracks of a hardboiled egg between one's hands like a trumpet, separating it from its shell in seconds like snake skin. Convenient for when eating on the run.

"You ran that fast," Andrec says to me about my mileage. As if to say, too fast.

"So you're the college kid from Washington?" he continues, wiping the dashboard clean with one hand. Cluttered between the windshield and dashboard and nooks inside the van are people's eagle and hawk feathers, beads, sage, and tobacco. Andrec keeps a secret stash of chocolates under his seat. Now he offers me some. "How's everyone treating you?"

He's Apache coming from Fresno, California, where he cares for his mother. He never knew his father, who left them when Andrec was a boy to live in Mexico. This is his second year on the run and the first time as coordinator with Pacquiao.

"People don't seem too happy to have me here," I tell him.

With chocolate in his mouth, he says, "Give them time."

✦

Again and again the work of the run is repeated. Runners are picked up and dropped off until someone says stop—that's either Andrec or Pacquiao. The van continues to swell with runners: Cheeto, Zyanya Lonewolf, Chula Pepper, Refugio, and others, climbing into the back of Andrec's van until there's no more legroom. We guzzle water and consume salmon jerky from Alaska. These are our snacks, which are stored inside coolers inside the vans, apart from gas station snacks and potlatch foods like fry bread, fish, potatoes, legumes.

"Little man, get in the back seat," Tlaloc says, opening the passenger door. He insists that I jump out and squeeze into the back seat next to Zyanya Lonewolf and behind Cheeto and another runner named Chenoa. I move back with the rest. The roof of the van is tagged with art, symbols, quotes, and inside humor. Messages to inspire, and remind us of why we do what we do. The van struggles up steep inclines and now and then, everyone gets off to jog behind the van until it can carry our weight again. In a quiet moment, all of us in our seats, I turn to Zyanya Lonewolf, who seems the most approachable.

"You've been here long?" I ask her.

"No. It's my first day."

"How'd you hear about this run?"

"Four years ago. The run came through my community," she says. "It was Chenoa who convinced me to join." They're from the same communities. Zyanya Lonewolf, from

Smithers, Canada, has lived most of her life with her grandparents, who survived the boarding-school system that fragmented their community, and younger brother. Her parents battle alcoholism. She has lived off the land, without electricity, and learned to tar roofs, build canoes, and prepare smoked salmon and animal hides.

Tlaloc blasts the radio and, sticking his head out the passenger window, shouts war cries, his long hair swaying. They give me chills. This man knows how to be free, I think to myself. His shouts remind me of the aipas that united my coworkers in the warehouses.

Tlaloc was born in a land that marked his spirit like a birthmark, on a small beautiful ranch in the state of Durango, in the Sierra Madre Mountains in central Mexico. His family had had great difficulty crossing into the U.S., and when Tlaloc was an infant, his parents made a third attempt in which part of their plan was to clothe Tlaloc in a dress. The family settled in East L.A., where six more children would be born. It was the perilous journey of their parents' migration that Tlaloc would grow to become most proud of, his parents' courage to risk everything. He is a beautiful man. Like Refugio, he tucks his hair back into a bun and wraps it in a neatly folded bandana just above his eyes. This man is pure power.

"Okay. Next runner," Andrec announces, braking and waking some of the others. Everyone jumps off for a quick stretch. The larger van is stationed beside us, where Trigger sits behind the wheel. "Noé. You start again from here," Andrec says.

This will be my second run of the day. Ten more miles.

The runners cram back into the gray van with Andrec. My muscles have cooled and stiffened. My legs quiver with exhaustion. I hide the pain. My shoes give me little comfort. I try to stretch, but as soon as I catch Trigger's eyes upon me, I start my run through gravel road immersed in thick forest, similar to before. The land abounds with green. I don't want him thinking I'm weak. For a while I keep ahead of the two vans that struggle around potholes dug up by the rain and now by my feet. I feel the power of an audience, eyes watching me from behind, wondering who this new runner is, evaluating me, my spirit, my running form, maybe wondering if I have what it takes to run five months and reach the finish line at the Panama Canal. Already I'm feeling the pain of a runner. The gray minivan is first to leave and slowly maneuvers beside me on the left, with all the runners inside, to drop them off in intervals again, while Trigger is tasked with driving ahead in the second van to wait by my mile marker, picking up the rest of the runners. I try not to let the pain of my sore muscles and blisters show.

"All right, little man. *Mexica, tiawi!*" Tlaloc shouts out the passenger window of the gray van as it drives ahead of me. "Mexicans, onward!" in the Nahuatl language. The gray minivan disappears, leaving me with Trigger scanning me from the bigger van. He drives slowly beside me, one hand on the wheel, the other under his chin. He glares at me.

"Everyone pulls their own weight around here. Got it?" he warns me.

I nod. To him, I am extra weight. A rookie needing to be put in his place.

"This isn't a game."

"Got it. I'm here to work. Really. I'm eager to learn," I say between running breaths. He smirks and speeds up, the vehicle's wheels further stripping the earth, and it quickly disappears down the tree-lined road. It's clear to me now that, at least unofficially, Trigger has a role managing PDJ. He acts like a leader, or perhaps a bully.

I punch my arms into the air and beat my chest like I did along the Naches River—reviving this human flesh into action. The wind cracks branches around me like a whip whipping me into shape. In this isolation I take the opportunity to shout it down, to scream at the ugly things inside of me as loudly as possible. I yell to make my speech physical, to give my words muscle, and to build the strength necessary to speak the things I never could.

I run to follow as closely as I can the path of those who came before me—migrants who knew suffering and deprivation. I run to find fragments of my own parents sprinkled over the earth, artifacts, their stories of hope and desperation. In facing these things, I try to finally bring an end to the suffering that has haunted me in childhood. I want to learn how to embrace my past, where I came from, and to love myself again.

I am finally, I feel in this forest, on a path toward becoming free.

8

Tree Noodles

While other people's fingers trace over maps on the hood of Pacquiao's jeep, on a hill overlooking Alkali Lake, in Canada's British Columbia, I open my tin of Tiger Balm muscle ointment. I lather it over my knees, letting it prickle. The smell alone is resuscitating. Before me, the lake's pristine waters are wedged between shards of steep mountains. Pacquiao, Andrec, Chula Pepper, and Trigger are in a huddle with a local elder from the small town of Clinton. They're charting a route through the mountains via an old trader's road. It is said that only a few elders know how to navigate it by heart. The elder from Clinton is one of them.

Among us since Prince George has been another mysterious figure who has appeared more comfortable in the shadows than in the sunlight. A man by the name of Marx, dressed in black, with clothes imprinted with the red star of anarchy. A person, I would later learn, who is former military. He, in his thirties like most of the others, often postured in the company of Trigger and Tlaloc, a clique of alphas keeping everyone in check. I have heard that he has had run-ins with women and Cheeto since Alaska. People he has cut down with insults, provocations, and intimidation.

"Whatever you do, stay away from that guy," Cheeto warns me. "Dude's not well."

A new girl appears: seventeen-year-old Crow. She has piercing black eyes and long black hair tied into a ponytail. News of the run had come to her through her sister's husband, who ran in 1996. The night before, she had gotten cold feet about joining. Crow had informed her parole officer of her plan to join the run, and had persuaded the officer as well as herself that it would be a good thing for her. But fear overtook her, and she hid in her favorite hiding spot in the woods. A cousin who knew where to find her caught up with her and convinced her to leave home for the sake of her mental health. It's been nearly a year since the death of her baby, and a year of living off the land in the woods, healing among elders who were helping reacquaint her to the old ways—fishing, hunting, and gathering medicine.

We gather around for Circle, where Pacquiao gives final word and direction. Like a sports team huddled around a coach, soldiers at attention, or worshippers at a church, Circle is a time to check in, talk general logistics, pick up staffs, dance, sing, and bring minds together in sacred reflection. They can last anywhere from half an hour to several hours. It is a time when the feathered staffs are picked up in the morning and put to rest at the end of the day. Circle is also a time for conflict resolution, a place for all to have a say, often lasting for hours and passing well into midnight.

"Brothers and sisters, today we run through the Lillooet and Mount Currie territories—beautiful and tough territories," he says. They are communities along the Fraser River, situated among deep gorges about 150 miles north of Vancouver.

"Before we move on, let's remember why we're here," Pacquiao continues. "We're here because we've made a pact with the land. To live in nature in a way that is not disruptive." An act that is done through running and that takes time to develop, he says. It takes time to plug into the land. "When you plug into it, it is strong, beautiful. But in many ways we're still not there, not strong enough to be there." That's why we run. I worry he's considering eliminating some of us from the run.

"Many communities are still trying to bring up their spiritual strengths, unearth themselves from the traumas of the past," he says. "That is why we use staffs." The staffs are works of art. They symbolize prayer. "They are instruments so powerful that sometimes it takes several people to wield them." Pacquiao points to the large paddle staff of Washington State, gifted to the run four years prior, and representative of the Canoe People.

After Circle, Chula Pepper tells me about her connection to the run. "If I hadn't met Pacquiao, I wouldn't have participated in PDJ," she says. "He pulled me in." They had both done philanthropy work in San Francisco, organizing for the PDJ. Chula Pepper was turning thirty years old, and, she tells me, "I was getting out of a relationship with a woman." She had nowhere to go. No job. Everything seemed to converge on one option. PDJ. "I identified as a gay woman in a Mexican community, if you can imagine," she says. Her words give me relief. People's paths are unique, beautiful.

"I really trust Pacquiao," she tells me. "He knows my own issues around being a second-, third-generation Mexican. My anxiety about fitting in—'Not white, what are you? Not really Mexican, what are you?'" She struggled with identity, had difficulty transitioning into Chicanx/Latinx communities and had a breakdown over it, and the meaning of *Mexican*, she says.

"I was raised Catholic, went to private school, and my dad was part of Knights of Columbus. I played sports," she will outline for me. "I had two younger sisters. I was part of the smallest Mexican family in my neighborhood," she laughs. "My parents divorced when I was eight years old and my mom became a single mother. After that, I went to public school mostly among Portuguese and Mexican classmates who didn't include me because I had grown up sheltered. I didn't have much cultural awareness," I will learn, and she will tell me about her first encounters with Mexican *cholas*, gangsters who chased and beat her up in junior high for growing up in a suburban white area. "'What are you anyway?' was people's favorite question," she will say.

Like in many of our communities, there is certain stigma associated with one's appearance. "My grandmother would always pinch her nose in the mirror," Chula Pepper says. "One day I asked her what she was doing and she said that she was missing cartilage and wanted to give herself a pointier nose." Chula Pepper pushed against this narrative. "She was ashamed of her looks."

She trusts Pacquiao and believes in what he is doing and his vision of what PDJ should look like. Finally, there is a place for her.

Pacquiao, Andrec, and Trigger finally organize the runners into action, including our new team member, Crow. As they gather equipment and load up the van, someone from Crow's community catches up to her and hands her an object: it is a small feathered staff, in honor of her lost baby.

We drive a short distance to where the old, dusty trailhead is—the start of today's run. Pacquiao and the elder from Clinton have driven ahead to meet runners at certain intervals on the trail and to steer us in the right direction since we are in tricky territory. The elder, I overhear, is one of Crow's teachers. He's a man born of this land, Crow says. He lives in a cabin he built himself, with no electricity. He taught Crow everything about drying and cutting meat, hunting grouse, and getting medicine from the land. He taught her about "tree noodles."

"They're harvested in the spring by peeling the inner bark," she tells me. "You run your knife down the side and you fill up your bucket." They're found in jack pine trees and balsam firs. "In old times, they were used as markings—for establishing direction, like the north. For when Indigenous families traveled on trails, migrating, to know where they were." She talks about how this elder from the Clinton area liked to put noodles on his plate like spaghetti and that, though he's still very traditional, he eats a lot of sugar. "He dips all those noodles in the sugar. Hangs them over the poles over the smoking rack until they dry hard. They're used for when you're out hiking. Survival food." But, she warns, eating too much of them causes stomachaches because the noodles expand in the stomach.

I am among the first people to run today, and I'm eager to expand my spirit and prove myself. When possible, I try to volunteer for extra mileage, trying to take in as much natural beauty as possible. It's better than being cramped inside the vans. I try tagging along with Tlaloc and Refugio—strong runners who seem deeply in touch with the spirit of the land. They talk openly to it, sing to it. I am eager to learn from them, to see what others see, and be fearless in nature.

I follow Refugio and Tlaloc's lead, into trails that are steep, windy, and rocky, trails that are like deep gashes in the earth. They move expertly through tunnels of foliage, ducking around boughs that brush and mark me. Our feet kick up earth that probably hasn't been disturbed in ages. We maneuver through overgrowth and over rolling rocks, our movement increasingly taking the form of the wild animals writhing within us. I try taking it one manageable step at a time, doing my best to focus on the ground before me and banishing any fears: Will I get lost? Can I surpass ten miles? Will I encounter predatory animals?

The land opens momentarily, where Pacquiao and the Clinton elder wait inside the vehicle. I welcome the sunlight warming my shoulders.

"Keep going," they instruct us, giving us further direction, then driving away, leaving me to trail behind the faint sounds of Refugio and Tlaloc's singing.

9

"Indian Time"

Lillooet Nation, British Columbia, Canada.

Zyanya Lonewolf, who is becoming a good friend of mine, wraps a bandana around her wrist for collecting sweat, ties her hair back, and puts on a visor cap that she picked up from a donation pile somewhere. She, along with Kara, Crow, Chula Pepper, Chenoa, and others, leads the run forward in a collective pace for a mile or two before hopping back into the vans and continuing the run individually, in the order of relay at about ten-mile intervals.

The path is perilous here. We run along winding highways, where trucks accelerate dangerously close to runners, causing Zyanya Lonewolf to hop to safety in the brush, or skirt dangerous precipices.

"Drivers are trying to hit me," Zyanya Lonewolf says to me after hopping into the van. "I jumped to get out of the way." She catches her breath. "I can tell it was on purpose. Damn truck sped up."

It is here that Zyanya Lonewolf starts to have doubts about continuing on the run. There's a long history of violence against Indigenous people here, high tension between tribal members and locals, dating back to displacement, the abusive residential-school systems, the string of murders spanning from the 1970s, and the missing and disappeared Indigenous women along the Highway of Tears. She tells me how racism is rampant in these parts of town and that it's frustrating that the women need to be especially careful. "You, too, eh," she concludes. "Getting hit by a car here would be no accident."

I knew that running wasn't going to be easy.

In the bathrooms, in her tent, and in the privacy of the trees near our camps, Zyanya Lonewolf does what she calls, "mirror work"—having motivational talks with herself in a mirror: "I love you, Zyanya Lonewolf. I love you, Zyanya Lonewolf." It is a belief among her people, she says, that intense fear can take away one's spirit, to the point of death. In such cases, it is important to call it back: "Come back, Zyanya Lonewolf, come back." All of a sudden you feel warm, she says. "I love you, Zyanya Lonewolf. You're doing the right work. I can do this. I can keep going."

✦

Finally, after many long hours, the run comes to a huddle on the outskirts of the Lillooet Nation. It is a land that opens onto a great canyon valley of wildflowers and horses near the Fraser River. Bulbous clouds filter the sunlight. The finish line to Lillooet is near, the elder from Clinton tells us. Only ten minutes, maybe fifteen or twenty, he says, and almost everyone hops out of the vans to attempt this last stretch into town together.

"Those who want to run the rest of the way into town should get off now," Trigger announces, and it's here that I learn the hard way what people call "Indian time"—an unreliable estimate in time and distance that often doubles, triples our runs.

✦

"We'll drive ahead and set up camp," Andrec adds.

It's the natural order of life, to run together. Carrying our communities forward, people run in one tumbling ball of high spirits behind the women, in a formation that restores my energy. We charge over land where horses graze, some of us singing. Tall grasses and a rainbow of wildflowers sway in the wind, turning the land into a kind of ocean of floral impressionism. I hold back, watching Nature's brush strokes at work even upon its spotted horses feeding and observing me from behind wooden fences. I'm downwind of them and can smell their hides.

Later, applauding families, little children, and hand drummers line the streets of Lillooet for our arrival. In a throng of singing women with their fists held high into the air, traditional music all around, we are led to a sacred hill for Closing Ceremony. There, where the air smells of sweetgrass and food, the community gathers in a large circle. My stomach grumbles.

✦

I learn there that the song the women have been singing is called the "Woman Warrior" song, written by a local Lil'wat woman who was imprisoned for defending Native lands.

"Like our sister who endured years of imprisonment for defending her homeland, we stand here today in similar cause. Now, more than ever, our mother needs us," a community leader says. Some people hold their staffs to the sky. Others kneel down to the earth. They talk about what plagues our communities—poverty, substance abuse, displacement, and oil extraction. "It is women who have sustained our communities, and it will be women who will bring back life into our lands," one speaker concludes.

✦

My mother—referred to by her sisters as *la Chiva Güera*, "the White Goat," due to her light complexion, was born in Coahuayana, Michoacán—living there some forty days, before her father moved the family to El Paderón, then to La Placita, where they lived until she was ten years old, and finally to the neighboring state of Colima. Colima was where she put down roots before leaving for the U.S. at the age of fifteen.

She lived in a rancher's and businesswoman's household—her dad dealing in cows, and her mom selling whatever she could, mostly food, out of her house. From a young age, my mom went door-to-door selling her mother's tamales, breads, and candies.

"I was good at this," my mom often said proudly. "I could sell everything my mom gave me to sell."

She talked happily of living in her quaint home down a cobbled street, within turquoise walls, with her two sisters. They lived there as domestic help, were taken out of school to work in their mother's shop, cooked the dinners, retrieved the tortillas, bought the produce in the markets, and washed the clothes.

Her mom had put her on a bus in Guadalajara for Tecate, Baja California, to then be taken to a brother living in Cowiche, Washington, thirteen miles from Yakima, where he lived in an overcrowded ranch house, decrepit and rat-infested, on the property of the orchard owner who worked them long hours. Her job, it was determined without her consultation, was to care for her brother's two children, while she lived among strangers in one corner of a living room partitioned with blankets.

My mom rarely spoke of Mexico with me. It was probably too painful for her to talk about how she immediately regretted coming to Yakima, having had a happier life with her family in Mexico. It would be many years before she disclosed to me her labors planting pines in the mountains near Yakima and having all her wages taken by her brother. After about two difficult years of struggling this way, she left her brother's house while he was away at work, to live with a cousin and his wife, people who helped her raise and save money picking apples. Despite her brother's threats to send her back to Mexico, my mother stayed, and survived.

Thirty years later in Yakima, when I see my mother sit in church, her parents now deceased, her milky white hands clasped together in prayer, I kneel beside her, wondering if she thinks it was worth it all.

✦

In Lillooet, the community distributes corn, fry bread, and buffalo. I fill my stomach. The children play and look upon us inquisitively. It will be their turn one day to run. As it grows dark, and the festive meal carries on, Zyanya Lonewolf of the Wolf Clan People shares a moment with me. She tells me why she decided to join the run. Her cousin, Ramona Lisa Wilson, a close and dear friend to her, was murdered along the Highway of Tears. Ramona was sixteen years old and one of twenty-one women whose lives were taken on that stretch of highway. This death haunted Zyanya Lonewolf. It is for her family and her cousin, the disappeared women, that Zyanya Lonewolf runs. It is a stand against the injustice, violence against women, and a move to take back the streets.

Her parents are survivors of the residential schools—the network of government-funded programs in Canada, administered by Christian churches, that removed Native children from their homes for the purpose of assimilating them by force, depriving them of things like their language, culture, and exposing them to abuse. "My dad had a lot of problems with alcohol," she says. "When he would get drunk, he would talk to me. He'd get real sad and tell me about residential schools and about what had happened to him." He was taken away from his family, he and his siblings, at the age of four, she said. His family had no say in the matter. "He would cry. He never cries. Barely smiles or shows emotion," she says with difficulty. "He's a blank wall usually. But when he would drink he would tell me traumatic stories." My father would sit me down in a similar way as a kid. Regular lessons in the hard life of our parents. "His parents had fought and fought for him and his siblings to come home. But they were given only one child of the three." She sighs before continuing, "They would starve them in school. They had a huge garden, and the children picked things like carrots and potatoes but never got to eat any of it." When she tells me that her father used to hide vegetables in the coals of the fireplace so that he could sneak out in the middle of the night and find carrots and potatoes in the coals to eat, my heart breaks.

The run does not lack for stories like these, and these are the stories that move me to run even harder.

"They starved them," she says. "I think that's why many

of us are unhealthy and overweight now. When people like my dad escaped residential schools, they ate everything they could. It was a survival mechanism, as they lived in fear that food wouldn't be available another day. Future generations packed on weight to have a better life, a better chance of our children surviving."

When her father finally came home, the damage had already been done. His parents worked hard to bring him up in the traditional way—a practice that brought back some healing to some people in the community, but not her father who did his best to teach Zyanya Lonewolf about this history.

"I wasn't shown praise or affection from my dad, but deep down I knew that he loved us." Love was him teaching her how to shoot a gun, she says, or how to identify different trees, how to cut them down to make a fire. Things that had helped him with his trauma.

She tells me that living off the land saved her life, and I wonder about the ways in which the land has saved my parents in Yakima. "My father taught me to never be afraid of the truth," Zyanya Lonewolf concludes.

10

La Cruz de Campos

My father was birthed in a house fashioned from mud and sticks in an arid land still unrecognized by many maps. There, in an impoverished town tucked between the folds of steep, sweltering mountains, among two siblings and his single mother, Guadalupe Campos Dominguez, my father got his start in life.

At eight years old, he comes up the rocky trail on his donkey, accompanied by his three dogs running ahead—Pololo, Titan, and Cutri. He unloads two buckets of water collected from a gully.

"Any news from your father?" his mother asks.

None.

Weekly he'd been sent to make inquiries at the post office in town, three hours away by donkey—that is, when the stubborn thing agreed to walk. Had his father, who had been away many years in Los Angeles, California, given any sign of his returning—letters, money, anything?

Nothing for the starving family.

They gather around for dinner. A single tortilla. The boy, seeing his mother separated from them in the corner, approaches her and asks, "Mom, you're not eating today?"

"*No, mijo. No tengo hambre hoy.*" No, son. She caresses his face. I'm not hungry today, she says, and encourages him to eat without her.

A boy never forgets something like this.

That boy, my father, was of a spirit born of hunger who has been forever defined by the pangs of an empty stomach and the mindset that if you don't fight, you die.

This boy often canvassed the bush, high in the mountains, in search of things to eat, looking for help in a land that wouldn't help him. He collected sapodilla chico fruit, captured birds and iguanas to take back to his family, and spent entire nights on the shores of the Pacific Ocean hours away in search of turtle eggs.

"I went out on rainy nights," he told me once, because turtles come out at night. Having filled his stomach, and too tired to make the trip home, he'd slip into a culvert to sleep—where he felt most protected. He learned to fish for crab, casting pieces of iguana meat into the ocean, and reeling them in. "The crabs attached themselves to the meat."

Sometimes, his mom sent him to ask neighbors if they had extra feed for their pigs. When people did, it was foul. "The worst tortillas."

"We didn't have any pigs," he finally admitted to me.

It was around this age of eight that my father found his first job handling fiery chiles on a chile-pepper farm. He remembers with joy running every pay day to purchase harina and masa for his mother.

"For the first time in my life we could all eat enough tortillas and with chile," he said.

11

Glacier Dip

Mount Currie, British Columbia, Canada. Roughly 430 miles from Prince George, B.C., Canada (via Alkali Lake and Lillooet). About 130 miles left until we reach the U.S. border town of Blaine, Washington.

Somewhere on a mountain, near Melvin Creek, is an elderly man who lives alone in a cabin. Hazel of the Stetliem Nation. He is reoccupying his land, he says, fighting timber mills denuding the land and ski resorts making preparations for the Winter Olympics. The Olympics devastate lands and displace people.

We enter the drafty, dark space of Hazel's home where dust kicks up at every step. Pots and pans hang from above and knock about like wind chimes. Native wool blankets faded of their colors but not of their people's magic, animal bones, and brittle furniture accentuate the room.

"I'm here to keep watch of the forest," Hazel says without any hesitation that he was brought into this world for the sole task of protecting the earth. He offers us the mulch of coffee that is as black and bold as the wet soil to enrich our spirits. The runners take their seats wherever, sipping in his words.

"Mother Earth is crying harder than ever before. It's time we listen to her, to her animals, to our surroundings. She's been crying for a very long time," he says. Native Americans have no economic strength, he tells us, because "we have to buy the land that was stolen from us."

I swallow the last of my coffee, rinse the cup, and step out into a mist that chills me to the bone and that reveals the watermark that is Tlaloc engaged in a private moment with nature, seated on the hood of the van, under a poncho, cross-legged.

"Can you please move?" he tells Chula Pepper, who happens to walk by. "I'm trying to see something beautiful."

After a gang conflict left him with a bullet wound in his leg, Tlaloc relocated to Arizona to live with an uncle. But while in L.A., his family believed that he had fallen in with criminal organizations. They believed that he was arrested for extorting money from people he preached about helping. Immigrants. That he had exploited undocumented workers looking for jobs and mediated for employers looking to employ them.

From an early age, Tlaloc hustled, went where the job

opportunities took him and wherever he could make a quick buck. The nine-to-five workweek was never an option for him, a brother of his would recount.

He had purchased a police scanner once, and listened in the dead of night in his car for the police codes that alerted him to accident scenes. He raced through the streets of East L.A. in pursuit of opportunities to find representation for undocumented immigrants for lawyers who had unofficially hired him.

After some years in Arizona, Tlaloc returned to East L.A. a different man, tougher, changed in the eyes of his siblings, with the bullet and emotional baggage still lodged in his leg. Arizona had exposed him to new ways of dealing with gang violence. He had gained something of an activist mindset, specifically around Latinx and Native American issues.

In the 1990s, before Arizona, Tlaloc and a sibling of his discovered Islam. They found a brotherhood offshoot of Muslim men who at the time seemed like the only people canvassing the ghettos of East L.A. and helping keep youth off the streets during one of the most violent times in East L.A. history. It was a time when there were no youth groups, and when people were left to their own devices for survival. People created their own way because they had to. Everyone knew that it was only a matter of time before the gangs got to you and you became affiliated with them.

When the brotherhood handed Tlaloc and his brother a flyer, they were already starved for a reality that was different from what they were experiencing. They started studying with the Muslim brotherhood—as ghetto Latinos attending mosque, a brother of his would say. Accepted among family.

It was here that Tlaloc learned discipline.

He began thinking about Native beliefs, too, and adopted these beliefs as his own. He talked to his family about Mother Nature, and how he was strongly against barriers and borders. How humans belonged anywhere they wanted to belong.

But Tlaloc's path forward was not a simple upward arc. He'd formulated his worldview and had often come home professing ideologies as extreme as the life he was leading, and having shoving matches with his brother. Drugs believed to belong to Tlaloc would be found in their mother's house, and she would be imprisoned. Legal statuses would be revoked, including Tlaloc's, his brother said.

Tlaloc went on to work with several other activist groups, including the Brown Berets who organized around issues including farmworkers' rights and police brutality, and continued on a path that would finally lead him to Peace and Dignity Journeys.

◆

When Hazel walks us through his land to a spring, a water source still pure enough to drink directly from, we follow and dip our heads under the water for cleansing.

✦

Zyanya Lonewolf asks the water for protection—for us on the run, and for her father, in jail after a drunk-driving accident that left the other party paralyzed.

"My father often contemplated suicide," Zyanya Lonewolf says. "I knew him as a strong guy. Those schools messed him up really bad."

After Cheeto dips his head in the water, he tells me he runs in support of women like his mother, the only constant in his life after his father left the two of them in Mexico to move to the U.S., and his grandmother, a Native woman he never met.

We fill our water bottles with spring water and leave Hazel to his land.

12

Washington Gray

We cross the Canadian border into my home state of Washington, where everything looks gray. The sort of gray that makes one contemplative. I feel the power of the rain most strongly along the Olympic Peninsula, running through Port Angeles and Neah Bay on June 12, and more intensely when we reach the Quileute Nation territory in the village of La Push—a place that averages seventy-eight inches of rain per year. The village is on the edge of a rain-forest teeming with moss from floor to ceiling, teeming too with stories of Sasquatch. Along the Pacific shores where fishermen's boats ply, bald eagles, seagulls, otters, seals, and sea lions congregate on small islands of rock.

Here I recognize the ways in which running is transforming me. Through it, I am inflicting violence upon myself and my body, submerging myself in pain like I did when working in the warehouses alongside my mother, so that I may control the turmoil within me. But unlike any other labor, running relieves me of the weight that I should become better than my parents, my people. I still don't know that it is okay to be unexceptional, ordinary, unremarkable. That there is greatness and pride to being common, so to speak. But I am learning to believe that it is okay to be flawed, imperfect. Running is helping me to see that.

✦

I hear Chenoa and Andrec arguing over the Mohawk Warrior Flag, a feathered staff that Chenoa feels is representative of true revolution and wants to run with, and that Andrec feels is too aggressive a flag to be flown on the run. To Andrec, the flag clouds the mission of peace and dignity.

Tlaloc joins the argument and strips Andrec of the flag, supporting Chenoa. Because the staffs are believed to hold special powers—imbued with the spirit of ancestors, they are to be treated respectfully as if alive, as if we were in the presence of a relative or an ancestor.

Andrec walks off. The magic between a staff and a runner must not be disturbed.

The run proceeds through this majestic landscape onto the Rialto Beach trailhead. Cheeto, Andrec, and I follow well behind Tlaloc and his crew of alphas through what looks like an enchanted forest of luscious green trees, ferns, and exposed root. Sitka, spruce, and evergreens accentuate life here. The trailhead opens to reveal a marvelous ocean before a graveyard of fallen fossilized trees along the shore and turned gray by the water. The icy waves, furious and too terrifying for me to approach, rip into the sand like bear claws.

Suddenly, like the dozens of bald eagles and seals tearing into the flesh of fish along the marina, Tlaloc and Marx claw into Cheeto like carrion, unprovoked, putting him into a headlock.

"Back off, man. Chill." Cheeto struggles to escape. They throw him to the ground and Cheeto storms off cursing under his breath and massaging his neck.

Tlaloc, like many things he does, approaches the ocean without fear, strips down, and plunges into its frigid water like he belongs there. A merman. Others join him more timidly. Myself, I sit on a pile of petrified wood, watching the misty shoreline, fog, and frothy sea, occasionally turning back to see rain run down and blacken the cliffsides like mascara.

✦

At Closing Ceremony, the elder Ipana gives a few words of inspiration, English being her nonnative tongue.

"Yeah. Many times life is too hard for me. Physically it's hard." She takes long calm breaks between her words and frail breath. "We lack sleep, I know. I also really miss home and people at home." The run is a real challenge to everyone. "Up in Alaska, it's harsh, cold, and really hard conditions.

Our people there live just to survive. There's no extra stuff. We don't own extra stuff. We don't have that kind of time. We keep straight forward to survive. We lead village life. That's all I knew when I was growing up. My parents, really strict about protecting environment. Very strict about many things." She talks about how the run is helping her to see the many ways that her people are related to so many other cultures. "One of the reasons I decide to run, is my health is not that good. I know I'm an age where I might get diabetic. I think running will be good for my health."

She then discloses that she will leave us for Alaska because her people have summoned her back for work to protect the caribou—a lifelong struggle for her people. "They are like buffalo. Our food, our shelter. We used to live in caribou hides. They are our tools, our clothing, our way of life. That's who we are. We're a caribou people. They migrate through our country. That's how we eat good again. And that's threatened now. Taking away our way of life. Taking away our humanity."

13

Goldendale

A year into his new life in Yakima, in 1979, my father, then age seventeen, had hitched a ride to work in the hop fields in Moxee, Washington, when he was stopped and apprehended by immigration officers at a roadblock near the Kmart. He and my mother were already together and, upon hearing of my father's deportation, she went into hiding to live with my father's brother, Gonzalo, and his family.

"They arrested us, put us into a bus, then dumped us in Tijuana," my father told me once. There, in Mexico, he chanced upon a friend who had been deported from Yakima the day before. "He was hungry and had nothing to eat," he said. "I had only seventy-five cents. So I gave him a quarter to eat a torta."

They were alone, left to fend for themselves until they could put their heads together and devise a plan to return—he to his brother, Gonzalo, and to my mother. "We made arrangements with a coyote, that we told would get paid in Yakima. They took us across, then locked us up in a house in Los Angeles," he said. When the coyotes left the house to confirm people's contacts and payment, my father and his friends panicked. "I told my friend, 'We better get out of here. Now's our chance.' We were scared they'd hurt us when they found out we were lying and didn't have any money." They broke through barriers and escaped to a nearby gas station and hitched a ride with someone who also wanted money. "We all emptied our pockets and put together fifty dollars." Nowhere near the two hundred dollars the driver was asking.

My father labored for months in Mendota, San Joaquín, and Fresno, in California, looking for work wherever he could. "Three days here, one week there, we looked everywhere for work. Tried to raise enough money to get back to Yakima and your mom," he told me. Finally, he and six others—none with a driver's license—stuffed into a 1980s Thunderbird.

Just when they were entering the town of Goldendale, Washington, only seventy miles from the town of Yakima, a state trooper stopped them and asked them all to get out of the vehicle.

"This stays with me. 'Walk the rest of the way,'" the trooper told them, as interpreted by others.

"He kept the car, then pointed toward the city. For us to walk," my father said. He didn't understand a word of English. "We walked a long time until we got to a pay phone, and I called my brother." Gonzalo left in a dilapidated car not his own that along the way broke down and forced him to hitch a ride to where my father was. "Now there were eight of us," my father said, in need of a ride home. Finally they secured a ride in a car so weighed down that it nearly scraped the road.

From that moment on my father tuned into the network of the people, Radio KDNA, before leaving the house.

My father lived on alert in a crowded house with Gonzalo, his wife, and my mother near Kiwanis Park pond where, when my siblings and I were kids, we returned to feed the ducks.

Over the years, at my mother's behest, he worked toward achieving his citizenship after having had us kids—my older sister, younger brother, and me. And only after my mother secured hers first, a year before him. "I'm very grateful to your mom," he said to me. "If it wasn't for her, I wouldn't have pursued carpentry"—a training program for immigrants. She encouraged him to become the person he wanted to be. "I really wanted to get out of the fields."

14

An X-Man

June 22. Eugene, Oregon. Roughly 1,170 miles. Amazon Community Recreation Center.

We continue to slip in and out of society like ghosts in the night, connecting our hearts and minds with the land and the many tribal peoples who cross our paths every single day, carrying the heavy thread of the prayers of hundreds of individuals. We run through landscapes that are referred to by their original Native names. Reinvoking the power of a name. Landscapes that start to take the form of our traumas and offer some healing. My body is weary and time and place become one big blur on the run.

✦

Some of us are growing closer every day, becoming great friends. Zyanya Lonewolf tells me more about her life. At thirteen years old, she experienced her own spiritual stitchwork. She thought it was all over then, had fallen into a deep depression and had taken to swallowing pills and cutting herself. "I'm a suicide survivor," she tells me. When she was growing up, everyone around her seemed at the mercy of drugs and alcohol, and she had turned to drinking heavily after her assault at her grandmother's house. "My grandma's house was open to everyone and everybody," she says. "That's where it happened to me." She sighs. "I felt worthless as a kid and my grandma helped me get through it. And even though she never spoke much English, she always listened to me." Her grandmother reintroduced her to culture and took her to potlatches. "You're valuable. You're worth it. You have the right to live and be happy, I told myself," Zyanya Lonewolf says. "Life is a gift. I always thought I was a mistake because I didn't have anything growing up. People tell you you're nothing and after a while you start believing it."

✦

One night, shortly after Closing Ceremony, after the feathered staffs and conch have been laid to rest among blankets, and each runner has gone their way for leisure time, there is a confrontation.

"Man, what are you doing?" Cheeto shouts, pulling away his sleeping bag from Marx, who heaves thick spit onto it. Marx, looking angry, shoves him aside and returns to his corner to huddle laughing with Tlaloc, Crow, Chenoa, and others.

"You all right, man?" I check in.

"Yeah. Them *Hollywood runners* are just clowning around," he says, with enough emphasis for Marx to hear. Hollywood meaning: some runners choose only to run areas with the most media exposure.

"Whatdyousay, motherfucker?" Marx lashes back at Cheeto.

"Nothing, man, I didn't say nothing."

✦

I pop a can of tuna and join Trigger in his van to try to bond. I learn that, like many of us, Trigger is a person driven by a call to return to the land. But he embraces an older, more antiquated version of order and custom than most others on the run. He is as if in perpetual training to return by force to a simpler way of life in nature—a process accomplished only through pain and suffering and that he embarked on years before I met him. Today he fights to discard himself of "the stupid times," he says. The times he used to be associated with gangs in East L.A.

"Nowadays the elite don't shoot us directly, but hand us the guns and we kill ourselves."

There's sadness in his eyes. His hands were once well acquainted with guns. He tells me of the friends he lost on the streets to gang violence.

"When I have kids, they will be born in the manner of the old way," he asserts. In a forest, under a tree, on a mountain somewhere.

I listen to him with the same desire to be reconnected with that eternal pulse reverberating in the land. His voice carries the weight of wisdom covered under a layer of broken glass. A wisdom that draws blood. I too desired to retrace my origin story to a specific spot on this earth, a specific soil from which my people's spirit first sprouted its first words. To know where exactly, in what house and village, my people first yearned for freedom.

"All things require hard work," he says as my desire to believe in something spiritual grows stronger every day for me, especially as I begin to understand the power of the Native American imagination—that a person can be who he imagines himself to be, and that if he fails to imagine, he fails also to exist. So, when an elderly man of African American descent by the name of Exzelian approaches me, on roller skates, after Closing Ceremony in Eugene, Oregon, to foretell my future, he says, I am ready to listen.

"I'd been observing your ceremony," he tells me. His leashed black dog sits obediently beside him. "Where y'all from?"

"From everywhere," I tell him. "Alaska. Canada. The States. Mexico."

He refers to himself as "X-man" from the planet Jupiter—a strange man offering to reveal his "powers of prophecy" to me. I squat down to pet his dog.

"My dog reigns on the planet Saturn," he says.

A few runners gather around. Trigger steps forward and volunteers his palm, listening to Exzelian make general predictions about love, money, and happiness. Things that could be said about anyone, I imagine. Nothing too impressive. He pulls Trigger close and whispers something into his ear, prompting him to pull back in shock. With Cheeto he reveals embarrassing facts about his love life, and Cheeto too pulls his hand away.

✦

Hesitantly, I offer my palm. Like any other fortune-teller, I imagine, Exzelian makes generalizations about me and my future.

While tracing the grooves of my palm with his finger, he tells me something to the effect of, "Good prophets read into the future, but the best ones read into the past."

He hits on something, and his brows furrow. "You were drowned in a previous life," he tells me, "at the hands of the god Poseidon." His mind keeps mulling. "You will marry twice," and he proceeds to reveal my economic future and also alerts me to some epic flood.

"Drowned?"

"Yes. Be careful around water. The god Poseidon is after you."

Then, pulling me close for only me to hear, he whispers into my ear a secret known only to me at the time. I'm in shock. I don't know what to believe. He grabs my hand firmly, preventing me from pulling away, and reveals to me something else—the age at which I will die. He releases me and rolls away on his skates, calling to everyone, "Have a nice forever!"

✦

That evening we lay to rest inside the Amazon Community Center where I bond further with Cheeto, who tells me that a couple of days before my arrival, there was a death on the run.

"When you arrived, it was like a breath of fresh air for me," he says. He tells me that after the participant died, there was a feud between Trigger and Andrec in how the run ought to be organized, but Trigger had more pull and authority over the others. But he was a reckless leader and driver and endangered others' safety. In his opinion, Andrec was more reliable and worked hard at establishing safer running routes. Trigger cut corners, didn't appear to care if runners suffered, and he considered pain part of prayer.

✦

I hand-wash and wring dirt from my clothing in the bathroom before retreating to my sleeping corner of the gym to flip through elusive words in my dictionary that I weave into dreams and where I also have some money taped away between its pages.

15

Apache Medicine

Between the years of 1997 and 2003, Andrec helped teach the foundations of sweat lodge to prisoners at Avenal and California State Prison at Corcoran—a facility that housed high-profile inmates like Charles Manson.

"Twice a year we'd accompany a Native elder who worked at the prison. We would sing to them. We'd instruct them on how to build a lodge within themselves. What it means to handle the fire." Two times a year the prison grounds would reverberate with drum circle. "Our elder would help prisoners with things like getting the gangster mentality out of them. 'Have you made peace?' 'Are you making amends with your families? Or are you repeating the cycle?' These are some of the things that he would say to them." They helped make songs with the prisoners.

Andrec's singing, when he gifts it to the run, is beautiful. He doesn't share it often with the group, keeping it close, but when he does, it stirs up something inside of me and mixes into my blood.

"What do you sing about?" I finally ask him, afraid that an explanation will dissipate his magic.

"I sing traditional songs. I sing eagle, bear, deer songs. Round-dance songs to remind me of the romantic person I want to be."

✦

Song is his prayer, he tells me. "Prayer is about who you are. When I'm out there, I think about humor. When I think about humor, I think about my mom—quick-witted, serious, and also very funny. Laughter is what keeps us strong. I sing about the nature of growing up in a harsh world. The world can be harsh. That's why we must sing the pain away."

Later in the day, Zyanya Lonewolf calls a meeting—Circle, to discuss and quell the problem of bullying on the run. A whirlwind of hateful words rises out of us all. Others bring up issues of theft, sex, and drug use. Pacquiao outlines the rules of Circle and takes a neutral role in mediating the conflict. Peace and dignity is a group effort.

"The run has begun to lose meaning for me. It's losing its direction," Zyanya Lonewolf finally musters. She studies the conch between her hands. "We started one way in Canada, but have become something else entirely." She raises her eyes. "Some of us should not be here. They derail our energy, our cause." Guilt shows on everyone's faces, including mine. "You know who you all are. You bully, you divide. Our ancestors would be ashamed of what we've become." She surrenders the conch. Silence. The whirlwind subsided.

"It's true," Andrec adds. "The run loses direction every day and the aim of some has turned toxic. How do we intend to heal when there's a lot of hate between us right now?"

"PDJ is for the strong. If you can't handle a little joking, then go home," Tlaloc adds, gripping the conch like a football. "We are not in some fantasy land. The suffering is real. The people we meet have real problems, and we need the strongest runners to carry their prayers. Some of you—and you know who you are—are holding the run back. You eat what little food we have, drink up our supplies, and drag the run down. Some of you should have quit the run a long time ago. If anyone has a problem, maybe they should go home."

There are arguments about what it means to lead, to run, to be a true Indigenous warrior. There's no consensus.

"We could do better," Andrec adds. "I have a lot of elders who taught me right, taught me how to be a warrior. Like Daren William and David Alvarez—a Yaqui. Both of whom fought in Vietnam. They knew that to be a warrior was not about carrying guns or violence. It was not about tearing people down like some of us are doing here on the run." Andrec's words carry a lot of respect, but they are, I can see, grating on Tlaloc and Trigger. "To be a warrior is to know how structures of power work," Andrec continues. "It is to sacrifice and dedicate one's life and energy to something bigger and greater than oneself. I'm trying to do that here on the run, to move in a way that lets younger people take over."

Circle closes without resolution, leaving us to our old patterns. Trigger tends to the van, Andrec to his map, Cheeto to his headphones, Chenoa to her beadwork, Refugio to his smudging of the feathered staffs, me to my journal writing, and Zyanya Lonewolf to her Native stitchwork.

16

Cougar Country

Reedsport, Oregon. Roughly 1,260 real miles and 1 million imaginative miles. It feels like forever on the run.

The van stops and the boil of the gravel road silences.

Trigger peers through the windshield. "No roads up that way," he says. He looks up at the mountain range. "Someone's gonna have to run it alone."

Andrec, Cheeto, Zyanya Lonewolf, and the rest of us put our faces to the glass and try sizing up the mountain. Nothing but silence. Our bodies ache. A mountain is not something anyone's willing to take on this early in the morning.

"Noé," Trigger calls out.

I look up and see Trigger's eyes in the rearview mirror.

"You're up."

I don't want to be the guy who holds the run back. But, fuck. A mountain? The moment to prove myself is now. It arises quicker than I expected.

"Van will meet you on the other side," he tells me. "Take that path there."

An entire mountain all by myself? It'll take hours. But putting our bodies through hell is the norm around here.

"Good luck, bro," Zyanya Lonewolf tells me. My heart races.

I jump out of the van and into the cold air, a shock like arctic water, I imagine. I stare up at the ripple of forest, the scars of earth that my feet will help heal with prayer. No one knows how long the stretch will be, only that I should stick to the main trail.

"Hold my staff?" I ask Andrec while I do a quick stretch. It's better to keep the legs moving and circulating than to keep them crammed in the vans. He hands it back to me. I drink from a water bottle then throw it back into the van. Water drenches my face and chest. The runners look at me. To them, I'm still the new guy. My legs are still fresh but I have a long way to go before earning my place among them. I pocket some salmon jerky.

"You got this. See you on the other side," Andrec says, and slides the door closed.

Like many times before, the van drives off into the distance without me. It's an image I never get used to. I can never quite trust that the runners will come back for me, but I have to trust in the process. I take a breath of fresh air and shoot forward toward the mandibles of a mountain and into a tangle of dirt trails.

The path winds forever between tall, unrelenting cedars.

Grasses shudder against a light wind. Lances of light spear through the canopy of trees and impale my eyes. The warbling sounds of birds play tricks on my mind. Deeper in I go, and steeper I climb. On inclines, I lean my head forward for support. Trees thick with moss crowd around me, studying me studying them. Deer droppings spot the area.

The quick transitions through sun and shade warms my face and cools my body.

I take off my drenched shirt in hot flashes of open land and wrap it around my head. I dodge, hop, and zigzag along the jagged earth, like a deer, and plunge into darkness. My toes dig into my worn soles. But too soon I'm out of breath and I doubt if I can make it to the end. But everyone is counting on me, expecting me on the other side.

I finally tear free from the long stretch of dark forest pressing up against my chest and into a greener, kinder world where long braids of verdant hair curl down from the green skies. Thick tendrils brush up against my shoulders and usher me over the earth like a puppet. The mossy green earth softens the impact on my knees as I struggle to run.

Suddenly, near the crest, I come to an abrupt stop. Maybe one hundred feet from me, in the middle of the path, is a mountain lion whose home I have disturbed. It lets out a low snarl that plants me on the spot, and my body goes numb.

Frozen, my eyes keep with the lion's. Controlled breaths keep me alive. It whips its tail, ready to lasso me in. Monstrous paws move massive muscle. Sharp shoulder blades click into position. Its black mouth and white mustache widen—tasting the air and aura around me. Judging my worth. Nostrils wrinkling, whiskers bristling.

Its eyes are almost human, large, almond-shaped. Sad, almost. Like me. It hisses. As if to say, "Hear me." My heart muscle tenses, and I clench my fists around my staff and tighten my stomach. Rigor-mortis tense.

It postures lower to the ground.

This is it. It's time to be tumbled and eviscerated from this path like a mudslide, relinquished from this world by the mouth of a beautiful lion.

We are alone in a forest, encroached upon on all sides by a tumultuous life, and compelled forward by survival. But I project.

I then remember Refugio's advice for surviving animal encounters: "Thank the animal." It snarls again, and lowers its tail. It moves toward me. I step back. Again it moves. I step back. I turn my head behind me and think about running. As if I could I outrun it.

Trembling, I raise my arms slowly toward the sky, and shout as loudly as I can, "Thank you."

It doesn't appear to hear me.

"Thank you!" I say louder and louder until it moves away. I tear up. "Thank you!" I shout, as if speaking first words to my father and mother, whom I never thanked. The cougar seems to register this and runs up the hillside, behind a boulder, and for the first time in a long time I cry.

✦

When my father was an orphan in Mexico, three stray dogs befriended and bore the weight with him. His mother had died in an accident—falling from the back of a crowded truck on the highway—and my father, barely fifteen years old, grieved among the three dogs who coaxed the kid out of him when he was forced to grow up too soon. They shook him from his depression, nudged him to press on, and defined what was a short-lived childhood. They gave him warmth at night, and helped him track and retrieve food when he shot lizards from trees.

After some time, his father made contact from Los Angeles and made arrangements for my father and his two sisters to move in with one of his mistresses, in the neighboring state of Tecomán, Colima, until he could get them to the U.S.

It didn't work out and my father became a beggar in the streets of Tecomán until he secured a job, which he kept for nearly a year, on a pig farm near El Tecuanillo, Colima, feeding, castrating, and preparing pigs for slaughter, he would tell me.

During nights, he slipped into empty burlap bags of pig feed that he laid for bedding, and slept among the pigs.

"There were rats everywhere. Big ones," he said. Fat from all the feed. "They fought all night," scampering over him and causing him restless sleep.

✦

I gather what little courage I can, inhale the power of my father, and lunge forward despite the lion's presence hidden behind a boulder not far from me. I sprint onward in honor of my parents, and maybe that saves me, because the lion does not appear again.

✦

At camp, Pacquiao makes an announcement that only the strongest runners will be allowed to continue into Mexico, due to the limited resources. He informs the runners that in order to cover more tribal ground, the run will be split several times into inland and coastal routes. The first split will occur on Hoopa Indian Reservation and will reunite in Santa Paula, California. The run will then proceed as one unit into East L.A. before splitting a second time and reuniting once and for all in Guadalajara, Jalisco, Mexico.

Nervously, we turn over this information in our minds, and busy ourselves with chores. Some of us begin to clean the vans, where mold and history are growing.

We are all worried about getting kicked off the run.

Who goes and who stays will be difficult. We all have wounds to carry and heal.

17

City-Slicker Natives

July 3. East Oakland. Roughly 2,140 miles. Cheeto, Tlaloc, Andrec, Trigger, and Chula Pepper are happy to be in their home state of California.

Inside the van is a constellation of quotes, layered on with marker by many who have passed through this vessel. Thoughts and emotions materialized into words passed on by people connecting with the run. A collaboration of many months. Quotes such as: "If you live as you always did, you'll receive what you've always got. Live life with respect," "They may have cut down the tree, but the roots are still there," and "I am nothing and at the same time something." Amalgamations of quotes collected from different sources on the run, I imagine. "You have plenty of time to suffer."

✦

We arrive at our destination at a cultural center and our team gathers in ceremony with the community. Kirby, a male in a tank top, jean shorts, and long socks that come up to just below his knees, comes forward as a representative of his community. I can't make out his tattoos. His mind is focused on the smudge of sage swaying all around us as usual. His people bathe him with encouragement. It's as if he's preparing for a boxing bout.

"Today our brother Kirby has volunteered to lead the run," a woman in ceremonial linen clothing announces. "He's strong, fast, eager to bring healing to his community. He'll be taking you through tough places, through tough streets." Areas that need strong prayer. Strong runners.

Kirby is a former gangster who was marked for death by rival gangs. Still, he wishes to run with PDJ through these rival territories, as his gesture of peace.

"Too many of us are dying on the streets," someone exclaims. "It's up to us to change."

My legs are tired, very tired, but eager to step the steps of brave men and women.

"We'll begin our run from here," we're directed. The vans will meet everyone at our destination. "Stay close and good luck."

We form behind Kirby on the street, where a large crowd has gathered. Cars honk in support. Our collective heart pumps in our chests and over these streets. Refugio, Cheeto, Zyanya Lonewolf, Andrec, and I gather up front and shake off our legs in preparation.

Kirby is handed the Father Staff. He kisses it, caresses it, and speaks to it.

Suddenly, he bolts off. The runners scramble and are stretched like gum into a string formation behind Kirby. Refugio, Andrec, Cheeto, and Zyanya Lonewolf are close behind, but it isn't long before the space between us increases and the chain and line of sight is broken. There's no looking back for Kirby. He maintains his sprint, concerned only with what's ahead.

The run is real.

Kirby flies down streets, dodges cars and pedestrians. Traces sectors of his past,

Meanwhile, this is not our first run of the day, and I begin to lose steam. Still, we run for all the Kirbys. We are his backup prayer, a gang of spirit. We run for him and people like him, because, in many ways, we are him. The despair, the universal graffiti, broken glass, and youth huddled on street corners in search of family. The group stretches even thinner. Refugio, Cheeto, and Andrec have long dispersed or have fallen back.

Kirby cuts corners, detours through parks and alleyways, and zigzags like he's trying to lose us. Still, we proceed, catching only glimpses of feathered staffs that aid us through this barrio. The sky darkens, late evening approaches, and then night does. Dim street lighting provides little visiblity or comfort.

I stop, realizing I've lost them.

I've no idea where to go. I can't retrace my steps. No

name of the place we're supposed to meet even. I look around, hoping to catch a glimpse of something familiar. A landmark, runner, anything, but I see nothing. If there's one thing I know about growing up in a tough neighborhood, it's to always act and walk like you know where you're going. Look like an outsider and you might attract unwanted attention. So I keep running, falsely confident. I remember the joke: when in doubt, turn left. I keep myself to a pace, circle around a couple of bars and taverns where men shout indiscernible things at me. I ask a woman for direction, but she backs me into the street with curses and territorial hand gestures. I keep moving—aware that I might look like a crazy guy with a stick and feathers in his hand. No sign of anyone. Fuck.

Confused, lost, even a bit frightened, I recall my run-ins with gang members in Yakima who bullied and beat me up.

Then, my heart drops at the sight of a fellow runner. I spot another staff with those comforting feathers, and I bolt toward them until I am once again part of the current of runners. Family.

✦

We meet for closing Circle at the Intertribal Friendship House, where Cheeto maintains a big smile, having run through his hometown and now being feted by his community. This is ground zero for him. Where it all began.

"It was here that I learned that many runners were, like

me, Purépecha," he tells me. Mexican Indigenous people from Michoacán, like my own ancestors.

Food and massages are dished out to everyone's content. After we have retreated to our corners on the floor, under bright murals and inspirational quotes, Cheeto tells me about sleeping here the night before he joined the run.

"I remember going into the kitchen and making food for anyone who needed it. Someone made enchiladas and fry bread in the kitchen. I ate some beans, thinking I didn't know if I would get to eat this in Alaska."

"So many things were on my mind," he continues. "I was preparing for something I didn't know too much about. But I knew it was time for me to prepare my body for pain: like the discomfort of having to wake up very early before sunrise, as part of the rules of the run."

"Centers like these," Cheeto says, admiring the mural above us, "are what's true to the history of this city. I was raised in San Francisco, and like many of us, we were pushed out into the Oakland area."

The mural is of the Miwok and Ohlone Tribes, he explains—families weaving baskets under the sun. "This is a good place where people of this community come to learn. Especially for people who are recovering from addiction."

Before zipping ourselves into our sleeping bags, Cheeto concludes his reverie about wishing to live in a world that includes other worlds. "There's this Mayan word, *lak'ech*," he says. "Meaning, 'You are my other me.'"

18

Tlaloc in L.A.

East Los Angeles, California. Roughly 2,600 miles.

Today the run gathers around the crosshairs of an East L.A. street where Tlaloc's little sister Sylvia was killed by a hit-and-run driver years ago. He was five years old then, and she was four. The story went that his mother had gone shopping one morning while the two siblings slept. When Tlaloc woke to find the house empty, concerned, he took his sister by the hand to go searching for their mother. Tlaloc sometimes shared that he remembers feeling the pressure of his sister's hand as it separated from his and that he carries a guilt that his family would say has plagued him all of his life.

Tlaloc hands the Father Staff to someone and kneels over his sister's spirit outlined with his tears. He puts his hand to the hot concrete. One pulse. Trigger kneels beside his close friend, positions his drum, and they sing in the Nahuatl and Spanish languages, a song I first heard in Covelo, California, titled, "*Cuatro Ágilas*"—four eagles:

"*Tlasocamat, tlasocamat, tlasocamate. Teyeye ometeyeyo. Tlasocamat, tlasocamate, ometeyo. Heyanayeneyowe. Cuatro ágilas, cuatro ágilas, cuatro ágilas volaron en Aztlán . . .*"

Today I am reminded of the tenderness of both these men, warriors with seemingly impenetrable skins. They sing of flying eagles and call on them for support. Two beautiful men mending the hurt within them, unafraid to let their love wash over this street. We are invited into this pain. I had been wrong about them, and I realize that it is in the heartbreak and frailty of others where we heal and see ourselves as we really are. I had cast upon them my own mistaken notions and let that cloud my relationship with them. I had trouble recalling that maybe what drove them to be hardened people sometimes was the lesson of a troubled upbringing, as it has done harm to me. I look upon these men with admiration, as examples of the kind of man I would like to become, had people like me not been so side-swiped by trauma. My heart breaks for them. I make my peace knowing that they will never accept me into their circle.

✦

Before long, tension between Andrec and Pacquiao rises over the coordination of the run. They have a conflict over how to split the runners for a second time in order to cover even more sacred tribal ground (between northern Arizona and southern Arizona). Because Andrec would be leading runners who are outright rebelling against him—Tlaloc, Trigger, Marx, and others—he threatens to quit the run if made to lead them through the northern Arizona route.

Pacquiao storms off in his vehicle in frustration. Splitting the runners was a tough decision. Communities across North America are pressuring PDJ to visit them. Andrec had established deep networks with Native communities across the West Coast, Arizona, Colorado, and New Mexico. For Andrec, it has been a way of life to build a fire rapport with these communities and link with them again on the run. So it hits him hard to surrender a territory that he has spent years organizing for PDJ due to the rising internal divisions and conflicts on the run. People were expecting to receive him but there were differences between the philosophy of Sun Dance and the more pain-oriented members of the run (Tlaloc, Trigger, Marx, etc.)—people who were a breath away from breaking or usurping the run under the wave of the Warrior Flag.

A lot of the ceremonies are land-based and land-specific, Pacquiao would say, and traditional territories expected runners to comply with these ceremonies. But Sun Dance and *danza* are more international and many other communities don't have that. They have very specific and different traditions and the run has to adapt to that. PDJ could not be a monolithic group, Pacquiao argued, because Indigenous people are far from monolithic.

"Sun Dance is a commitment of prayer," Andrec had

said. "It is about understanding that, yes, you will be fasting and praying with very little comfort but that the goal is to seek inner self-awareness and respect. The pain of Sun Dance cannot be inflicted on people nor can you teach others by enacting harsh discipline on them." This ran in direct opposition to Trigger's worldview.

Andrec has a heart-to-heart with Pacquiao about his role to lead Tlaloc, Marx, Trigger, and the others into Navajo country—a land he greatly respected. "Let them go on their own," he concludes. "It's what they want. It will either make them stronger and more unified. Or it will break them." Tlaloc and the others had become their own band of brothers and sisters, more in the fashion of a gang and violent toward outside runners.

Pacquiao thinks about the proposed restructuring. "You know. You're right. We'll let them go then."

"It's better to lose them for a while," Andrec says. "They're gonna scare away the good runners." Tlaloc doesn't want to split from Crow, and takes her with him. Andrec gives up his chance to run through his sacred Apache land. A heavy blow to his heart and to the people who were expecting to see him.

Pacquiao returns the following morning with his final decision: The inland route will consist of Tlaloc, Crow, and others who will run to Phoenix, Texas, then into central Mexico, into the state of Chihuahua. Chula Pepper will stay back in San Diego to help with van maintenance. A group of local East L.A. runners have volunteered to run to Phoenix and Texas for support. The coastal route will consist of myself, Pacquiao, Andrec, Cheeto, Chenoa, Kara, Zyanya Lonewolf, Refugio, and, to Andrec's surprise, Trigger who had become romantic with Kara. Andrec is happy with the decision and stays on the run.

✦

In anticipation of crossing into Mexico, I find a phone and call my parents. I lie to them and tell them I'm living in luxury and am the happiest I've ever been.

✦

In the morning I take to my usual responsibility of loading up the vans and stacking people's gear onto the roof. Andrec assists me. We knee things into place and envelop them in a tarp like a tamale. Refugio's duffle bag rolls to the ground, and we hear what sounds like pills hidden inside. Refugio recovers his bag, zips it up, and hands it to me. Vitamins, he says.

19

Southern Fire

There are moments in a boy's life when he thinks a single action can turn him into a man and solve all his problems. I thought that moment arrived when I was twelve:

It's that time of day again when strange music flows from the old white house across the street on Jefferson Avenue, our neighbor Dallas's house, and into the small carpeted living room, where I sit watching through the curtains my brother Tito launch himself from a skateboard. He's eight. I'm twelve. It's midday, summer, in eastern Washington State in a poor neighborhood that keeps its doors ajar for cooling.

Our kitchen is fragrant with our mother's cooking.

"*Noé, acaba tus quehacéres,*" my mother says. Her hair is in a ponytail. One hand rests on her hip, while with the other she toasts red chili peppers as if to clear the house. I run outside to play with Tito, coughing, leaving our mother to stew in thought until our father arrives.

In the late evening after work, my father rests in the dining room, in his usual chair, beside steel-toe work boots that are crusted with dirt. An orchard laborer and carpenter grappling with a language he doesn't always understand, he pores over a stack of mail. "*Noé, tradúceme esto,*" he asks me to translate something and shows me a paper in English.

I look it over. Numbers, words. "I don't know what that word is," I tell him. I am too terrified to translate the words "bill overdue" for him.

At bedtime, I lie awake listening to the muffled voices of my parents fighting in their bedroom at the far end of the house. I remain quiet, brooding and bothered. Tito is on the top bunk. Soundless. An indication that he's not sleeping. In the distance, Dallas's keyboard soothes me to sleep. The quicker we become men the easier things will be.

At breakfast the following day, I quietly pick at my food. My parents make little conversation. A screen door slams across the street and a woman yells and curses. We turn to the window and watch Dallas toss the woman's clothes onto the front lawn while she collects them one by one. The screen door slams again and again, Dallas going in and out, each time coming out with a new bundle of clothes to hurl at her. I run to the window for a closer look but my father calls me back to the table. "Ignore them," he says, and gets back to mulling over more pressing matters. When the screaming and yelling finally stop, I stuff the rest of my food in my mouth, and Tito and I walk to school together.

When we come home from school later in the day we are surprised to see black trash bags filled with clothes piled in the living room. My father is home early, sitting at the dining-room table.

Without looking at us, he tells us, "Take those to your mother next door."

We remain motionless. We are told that our mother has gone to stay with a neighbor.

"And tell her never to come back. Go."

One by one we carry the bags to the neighbor's house next door. We knock on the door.

"Here are my mom's things," I say to the woman, and place them inside her door. I hear our mom sniffling in another room. I want to call out to her, tell her that I was sorry if I did anything to hurt her. Sorry that I wasn't brave enough to stop this. "Tell her . . . " My chest tightens. "Tell my mom to never come back." Those last words really choke me. My father's words had become mine and I became a perpetrator in the destruction of my relationship with my mother.

Our neighbor cautions us, "Be careful what you say. You'll end up regretting it your whole life." I immediately do.

✦

Again, later that evening, the block becomes heavy with the wails of a Dallas man who sways over an electric keyboard. Deep-bellied, measured, his voice braided in torment. The man crouches over his instrument and sings strange words of sorrow. His music grips me, notes that seem to punch him and me in the ribcage. He rocks his head back and around, blowing out soft cigarette smoke as if absorbed in his own church. These are the sounds of Southern fire, ignited by the hands of a man speaking in a language he calls the Texas Blues. A language that resonates with me.

Dallas goes by that nickname to avoid the law, or so he says, and is somewhat of a surrogate father to us. In a warped yellow house half the size of his, tucked in the same yellow grass, lives his neighbor and sidekick, Randy. Two Vietnam War veterans now living a life of sex, drugs, and music. We witness the parties, the brawls, inebriated bikers bathing with topless women in kiddie pools in the backyard, and the passing out on Dallas's front lawn.

The music stops and the screen door slams. Dallas walks out barefoot onto his porch in dark aviator glasses, a stained white shirt and shorts, and untangles a Texas flag from the front of his house. No wind to ruffle it. He scratches his belly under his shirt, strokes his handlebar mustache, and walks into the threshold of sunlight onto his front lawn with beer in hand. His long salt-and-pepper hair tumbles over his shoulders. He picks up a garden hose and squeezes flaccid city water from it over a flower bed of marijuana plants below the steps.

Randy ducks out from under the small doorframe of his house and walks toward Dallas, slapping a pack of cigarettes. Barking wiener dogs escort him at the ankles. Guard dogs in the troubled neighborhood. Randy shouts, they quiet.

Dallas calls out to me when I step outside. "Hey, ninja man!" and walks up to the edge of his fence, reaching into his back pocket. "Come over here, amigo," he says playfully in butchered Spanish.

I walk across the street while Dallas counts dollar bills from his wallet. Tito steps out.

Dallas sets his beer and wallet down on the grass and opens the gate. "Whatsup, you little *cabron?*" he asks. He puts his fists up, fighter position, play punching and kicking at me despite the pain in his hips. "Show me what you got, little man," and he puts me into a soft headlock, under his wet armpit that smells of the hops factories in town. The perspiration of beer. His toenails are cracked and yellow. My cheeks feel the abrasive callouses of Dallas's fingertips—the tips of a musician. "C'mon, is that all you got?"

Smiling, I punch Dallas in the belly and free myself, also getting into a fighter position.

"Here's the money I owe you from last month," he says, and hands me thirty dollars. "Can you mow my lawn today?"

I nod. Before I can run to collect my father's lawn mower, he stops me.

"Everything okay in the casa?"

I look down at my feet and force a tight smile.

"If you ever need anything, come to me, okay?" Dallas lights a cigarette and takes a long drag and long moment to look at me. "Tell you what," he bends down to my level. "Wanna make some good money?"

I don't answer.

"This is between you and me. No one else. Okay?" He tells me the plan. One that would make me big money.

The days are lonely without our mother and I find myself often sitting on the front steps with my brother, hoping our mother would turn up again. It's around this time that Tito really withdraws into himself, into his things in his room. Building gadgets out of collected trash, inventions, solutions to problems that no child could ever fix. Wings made out of cardboard, devices with wires, swords, slings, and weapons of sorts.

On the night that I will carry out Dallas's plan, I wait for my father to go to bed, then remove my bedcovers, quickly dress, and tiptoe through the house to a living-room window to inspect the night. All is still. I exit into the cool air and make a run for it through the street, around the block, and down through the back alley, as Dallas instructed me. The alley is unlit, tagged with blue and red graffiti. When I finally reach the garage, I pry the stubborn door open, and hide inside, where the air smells of gasoline. Slivers of moonlight penetrate the structure. There's no turning back now.

✦

I grab the heavy gas tank from where Dallas said it would be, and I clumsily pour it in and around the garage, until it's empty. A faint glow of morning pink creeps over the horizon as I stand outside beside the garage with a lighter in my hand. I turn, look at my blue house across the street, and finally at myself.

20

Man in the Maze

Ajo, Arizona. Roughly 3,000 miles. Tohono O'Odham Nation.

The heat waves in Arizona are suffocating and it feels like we are running through curdled air. We run eastward through dry country with salt pouches around our necks, which we dip into now and then to help keep us hydrated. The bottoms of my soles burn over the hot roads, so I run over the earth for relief, kicking up dust with horses behind me—tribal cowboys, Felix and Si, from San Lucy Village. The sunburning days coat me with dirt and doubt, and I'm not sure that I can go on. My friends are losing steam. Cheeto suffers from back problems and Refugio continues to rely on his vitamins to keep him going.

To beat this heat, we run in the early hours, from dusk to dawn. Some runners give up, others get injured, and the low water supply causes dehydration symptoms among several of us. But I am propelled forward. If my parents and other immigrants can endure treks into foreign lands, then I can endure a little pain. My struggle on this run is a small thing before the pain of my people.

We sleep less and less, and run more and more, desperate to pick up the slack of injured runners. We now average four hours of restless sleep a night, falling behind on mileage goals every day. One runner gets lost in the desert and a search party is sent out for her—further stripping us of our confidence that we will persevere. Water is low, Trigger tells us, though he continues to secretly store food and water from us. I watch him do it on a regular basis—he stashes water in compartments he built with wood, and locks up the van. I tell some of the others but it's not enough for anyone to confront Trigger about. He bullies me into running more, demanding that if I can't handle the run then I should go home.

Our destination: sacred Baboquivari Peak.

My struggle to run is alleviated in the company of the two horses who must also endure the journey. We're together in this. Like counting thunder, their hollow clip-clop over the road serves to measure man's distance in life, drawing out invisible obstacles that have been corralling and preventing man from achieving his full potential. The horsemen notice my pain and counsel me on the proper way to run.

"Man must learn to run like the horse, evenly and gracefully. Not too much weight on the toes or heels," they tell me.

I watch the grace with which their horses run, an empowering attitude toward life.

"The horse has brought much healing to our communities," they tell me. "It is because of them that we could hunt and trade over vast lands."

"But we do not own them," they continue. "We partner with them. We are equal in our quests."

For miles, the vans move slowly forward over the scorched desert as the runners jump in and out of the doors, left ajar for efficiency. No air-conditioning. Several of us, including Refugio, Andrec, and me, are taking on too many miles without proper food, water, or rest. Still, Trigger pushes us. Tensions mount.

"Get out and run, Noé," Trigger insists one day, when the van is empty.

"I'm taking this lap off," I tell him, massaging my melon-size knees. Sixteen miles already under my belt today, but in Trigger's eyes, we runners are not pushing ourselves hard enough.

He hits the breaks and turns around. "Get out or I'll get you out."

I grab my staff, sip the last of my water, and hop out. Dust clings to my sweat and my sunburnt shoulders hurt under the sun. I wrap my head in my shirt for protection and move forward as best as I can toward a van that quickly becomes a speck on the horizon.

Suddenly, a bolt of pain, like lightning within my nerves, strikes my knees, and I fall to the ground. But I know that I cannot stop now, that my marker is ahead, and that I cannot appear too injured lest the run decides to eliminate me from the run. I'm too deep in this life now. I'd be nothing without it. I'm close now, I think, to Mexico, where the real adventure is. Mexico, where it all started for my parents. It's there that I most want to run. There, where I most want to pray and where the stakes are much higher. With this in mind, I run and power through my pain.

Running, I begin to learn the hard way, is a sacred motion—different from the assumptions I had of the act growing up, when the stories I knew were only of migrants running from immigration raids, and mass deportations. That, coupled with my own experiences, back then, of running from street gangs. The motion of running to me meant a defensive act, one that arose from the fear and desperation of a vulnerable people who were running as a means of survival.

Running on PDJ is helping me to see my life and family's migratory experiences in a different light. To recognize its healing aspects, while also not overlooking the detrimental effects of it, like forced migration. It is a complex relationship.

Running is rhythm connecting me to the wind, the water, the woods. It is about "belonging to the land"—a value deeply held among Native communities. It's about performing the gesture that reminds us that there is always something bigger than us and to respect our environment. It calls on us to defend the land like we would defend our very own mother, and understand that we can never own it. I learn this in the act of digging my toes into the earth as I run barefoot through nature, attuning myself to vibrations bigger than myself. To run over the land is to run with attention.

For longer than I can remember, I was ashamed of who I was. I was ashamed for having no real sense of place or home, and it has taken this run across North America to learn that home is everywhere in movement. It is in my many steps that I explore my emotional replies to the land, different from how I experienced them as a small boy in the apple orchards where people like my parents were exploited for their cheap labor. I left that land thinking I'd never return to it for the stigma of what it meant to be a family of migrants in Yakima. And unlike those helpless migrants who tumbled from trees and dropped everything they had to run to safety, I ran away, knowing that I would do so on my own terms and with love—not fear. I would travel wherever I wanted, on my own terms. Confronting the unfamiliar and integrating the beauty of life with my very being. I'd conquer my fear of the unknown outside of the hills of Yakima.

The evening skies thunder and the heavy rains finally arrive. I strip down to my underwear and shower for the first time in days.

21

Running the Wrong Way

I've been on the run for what seems like forever when I reach the border town of Nogales, Arizona, roughly 3,200 coastal miles from Prince George, British Columbia, Canada. There, I come face-to-face with what has defined me my entire life: the U.S.-Mexico border. There is the absolute edge of my world; the border that splits me in two, between who I am in the U.S. and the people my parents were in Mexico. I approach the terrifying border, the swaths of graffiti, Spanish music reverberating from a long line of cars, and I present my U.S. passport to the border agent.

"What will you be doing in Mexico?" the officer asks me.

"Running." I have given up trying to explain why I am doing what I am doing. Running. Across North America. Grasping for freedom. With Native Americans. For peace and dignity. "To Central America," I offer.

The border agent raises his eyes at me. "What are you running from?"

No one has asked me this question before. "From nothing," I answer, still jogging in place, because those are the rules of the run: to keep running no matter what. No matter the pain, no matter the risk, or no matter how sorry one felt for oneself.

The officer flips through my passport again with more care, more doubt, then asks with a twist of humor in his voice, "But aren't you running the wrong way?"

I stop jogging and think seriously about the Latino officer's question. I hadn't ever thought about what was the wrong or right way to run. And now, when I need all of my courage to continue, when running matters most because it will take me into my parents' homeland, something swells up inside of me that causes me hesitation: Was I really running the wrong way this whole time, thousands of miles and nightmares later, in pursuit of my parents' past and to better understand them and who I am? I look at my knees—swollen like grapefruits wrapped in bandages, and I think about all the shit I put them through since dropping out of college and abandoning my parents who labored in the orchards and warehouses. My decision to run away from family dropped me into a life of daily, all-weather running, on a journey that is charted from Alaska to Panama where I camp outdoors, in community shelters, reservations, casinos, and eat mostly on the go like a fugitive.

I look deep into the dust-plowed horizon to the north

from where I came, into the mirage of all that I had conquered in my life laboring outside in *los files* with blistered hands, and am now conquering anew on blistered feet. Like my parents, I am a runaway from a life I didn't choose for myself. I searched desperately for meaning across North America, in the wildest of wild regions, in ceremony with tribal elders, some anarchist Natives, peyote, and predatory animals. I then look in the direction of the south, into the heart of the monster that is Mexico, and it fills me with terror. I tighten my shoelaces and look toward the land that my parents fled.

The time to quit the United States has arrived.

22

The Devil's Coffin

Sonora, Mexico. The early days of August. It's true that the land does not recognize national borders. My transition into Mexico feels familiar—nothing to distinguish it from the lands of Arizona, or even the desert of Yakima, besides the Spanish signage, archaic *pueblitos,* adobe structures, and undeveloped roads that sprawl from cathedrals, sacred centers of many Mexican towns. A lean man with long black hair, in seashell regalia and running shoes, receives us in Mexico, near the border. His name is Mazat.

"Hello, brothers and sisters," he speaks in Spanish. "It is an honor to receive and welcome you into our community." I feel that the run has shifted dimension again, plunged us into a world south of the border where the rules will be different. Where the food, language, and harsh terrain will test us. As Mazat speaks, his voice carries the weight of something spiritual. It reminds me of the voices of elders. "We are a people who follow the warrior path," he says. "Our names have never been erased by the weapon." I know then that Peace and Dignity Journeys would represent for me the beginning of a new tradition—to remember our place on this earth, to break away, by the drumming of our feet, from the rhythm of old patterns.

✦

Before we break into relay-style formation, en route to Punta Chueca via Magdalena and Pótam communities, Pacquiao selects two new Mexican runners to join us, Mazat and his brother Greñas. From Nogales we proceed through the municipality of Hermosillo, into the coastal town of Punta Chueca, through a rugged landscape of volcanic rock called the Cajón del Diablo, "the Devil's Coffin," and farther through the towns of Guaymas, Pótam, then into Los Mochis.

I take off on my first run in Mexico under the intense heat of the sun, along a highway lined with trash—yet this soil feels sacred. The day drags on and my knees are in agony. Sometimes I slow to a power walk, but I don't stop. My parents' history comes to me in the fragments of each step. It gives me the strength to push myself. Here my people will welcome me.

But this feeling is struck down by a rock thrown at me by a figure in a passing truck. It knocks the air out of me and I crash down. A man in the passenger seat flips me the finger and drives away to where he will do the same to other runners, leaving us welted and bruised.

We slip through one small town after another, as strangers through border communities scarred with violence: immigrant deaths in the desert, cartels, and corruption.

✦

Meanwhile, up ahead in the volcanic fields of El Tecolote Cinder Cone, Zyanya Lonewolf has been carrying the Father Staff over a road that seems to boil under our feet. This world looks like a coral reef. The rocks and boulders are large enough to dart behind, provide us cover during bathroom breaks, and we need them, with our upset stomachs, infections, and dehydration.

On this day, Zyanya Lonewolf, charged with leading the run for the day, gets lost. A fork in the road takes her down a barren dirt path and she pushes forward for miles. Far off in the distance she notices a group of laborers. She presses on, continues through a field of more and more rock, when from the bushes, a man jumps off his bicycle and approaches her, shouting something in Spanish at her. A language she does not understand. He grabs her arm and tries pulling her toward the bushes. Instinctively, Zyanya Lonewolf hits him in the face with the staff and runs as fast as she can in the opposite direction, back toward the highway from where she veered.

Some time later, Pacquiao's car finds Zyanya Lonewolf.

Pacquiao, seeing the lost runner holding the Eagle Staff, loses his shit. The Father Staff must always remain ahead of all the other staffs. Pacquiao is a two-hundred-pound man, a lifelong athlete who has been shaped by the codes and constraints of boxing, hard living, and community organizing for farm laborers in Arizona and California. Labor movements defined him. This was the man who threw a rage at discovering that a runner, the run, the greater vision of PDJ, had been assaulted. Pacquiao asks Zyanya Lonewolf to point him in the right direction, and he and Andrec chase after the guy on the bicycle. Zyanya Lonewolf runs the rest of the way alone.

The day grows late. Hours pass. Andrec and Pacquiao go farther down the road questioning anyone they see about a guy on a bike, while I and the other runners converge for Circle only to compare the welts on our backs from the rocks thrown at us.

Already Mexico is testing us.

23

El Chapito

We finally reach the Pacific Ocean, where the breeze gives us some relief, and the runners rest. There, we are greeted by an elderly Indigenous man from the Fisherman People of the Seri Nation, named Chapito, a shaman with deep knowledge of medicinal plants and of the old ways.

Chapito accompanies us on a motorized raft to Shark Island, where he was born. The raft bucks across the ocean while Chapito stands well-balanced on the bow. He rides it all the way while holding the Father Staff and singing. For a few moments, I forget my aching, swollen knees. This man, full of life, knows these waters well. Through tobacco smoke he sings the "Andaleteo" song, a song that describes the ocean's battle between happiness and sadness. Later, through an interpreter (Chapito doesn't speak Spanish), Chapito tells me that the road to happiness is also the road to sadness. "To be happy," he says, "one must be sad."

24

Deer Runners

Obregón, Sonora.

The van Trigger drives runs out of gas on the highway.

"Run the rest of the way, Noé," Trigger commands.

Trigger and I get into a heated argument about what it means to be a runner with PDJ and his rationing of water.

"I don't run for you, Trigger," I tell him.

"Like hell you don't . . ." He gets out of the van and opens the side door. He stands, waiting for me to jump out.

Quiet Kara, his love, sits silently in the passenger seat. Trigger threatens to throw me out of the van when I tell him I won't run any more miles for him, not until he gives me a water bottle.

After Kara sneaks me a water bottle, I rewrap my knees and take off on my run. Here in the state of Sonora, we are accompanied by police cars—the governor has ordered this, for our safety. So a police car follows behind me as I run. After a while, it pulls up beside me when I'm alone on the highway in the deep desert haze.

"You're hurt," a voice comes from within the car.

I duck and peer through the window. A strikingly beautiful policewoman.

"Why do you run?" she asks me. She must have noticed the irregularity of my jog. Like someone with a nail stuck to his foot.

"I have to," I say. I'm not good at anything else in life.

"*Eres Mexicano?*" she asks.

I hesitate, feeling I don't deserve the honor of such a label. "My parents are."

Her name is Victoria. She tells me that she's not like many others here in northern Mexico, who desire a life in the U.S. "I don't believe in the U.S.—that it could offer me anything better," she says. "My people and responsibilities are here."

Meanwhile, PDJ in many ways is disintegrating. Our relationship with local communities is becoming more strained every day. Here, the people's distrust of us demands that we work harder to be better guests. It's difficult to model behaviors of peace and dignity on an empty stomach, battered knees and soul, and beaten pride.

Later in the day, a local cowboy in flashy clothes who has been following us from Pótam approaches me in private to inquire about PDJ's purpose in Mexico. He asks why Mexican police are escorting us and he cautions us: "The community is watching." He does not believe we are running for peace, or anything good, for that matter. He thinks we are plotting political upheaval.

But there is good, too. Three Mexican soldiers have joined our run. They put their guns aside and pick up staffs to run alongside us. They fight the stereotype that all people in their line of work are corrupt. Today they surrender what symbolizes power—the gun—and they sweat for their people. Today will be a day without violence, though the threat of it is never far—after one of our women runners survives an abduction attempt, Pacquiao announces that women will run in pairs.

Victoria and I become more acquainted. In her acceptance of me, I begin to understand what it might mean to be Mexican, how my life might have been had my parents never left.

On our last day in Sonora, Victoria gifts me a cowboy hat for sun protection.

"Ahora sí eres muy Mexicano." Now you are very Mexican. She smiles, and gives me a peck on the cheek before driving away.

25

Chihuahua

In Chihuahua, some of the inland runners have settled onto a plateau overlooking the desert in circle formation around a fire. They have popped peyote buttons under the direction of a wandering medicine man, permitting their minds to become spindled with magic—minds laced with the intricate webs of hallucination. All night they sing, dance, laugh, and Crow and Tlaloc become closer. They dance until the stars close in on them, eliminating the space between the here and there. The fire and dances dwindle. Laughter becomes fainter as people withdraw into the pulpy atmosphere of peyote. Crow and Tlaloc sit under the stars when it darkens, forgetting to tend the fire pit. The peyote strengthens, and they connect over things of two people madly in love.

The morning finally comes and with it two horses. "C'mon. Get on," Tlaloc says from behind the reins of one of the horses, bareback riding.

"No. I'm too scared," Crow replies but eventually gives in, mounting the other horse on bareback, clutching it with dear life when it dashes after the other horse, on Tlaloc's tail, into a valley of brush along a creek. "I'm going to die," she shouts.

"The horses know the path by heart. You'll be okay," and they slow along precipices and ridges. Old trails carved out by animals. The walls of the canyon nudge them toward the center, into tighter spots. They come to a stop along the water, dismount, and skinny-dip into the water together.

When I wake one morning, I am sleeping on my stomach on a floor. Something has awoken me, and then I know it: a burning sensation rips through my back. I ask Chula Pepper to look me over.

"Oh my God," she says, backing up. "Here, you need to see for yourself," she continues, and brings me a mirror. I see blisters all over my back.

The locals help me determine that it was cricket urine, bugs that nested on my back all night.

26

Touch of Treasure

I lean over my dog over a pool of my blood. My shoulder is red with the blood dripping from my lip where my dog bit me.

We used to have a dog, my little brother Tito and I, in Yakima. A German shepherd named Tesoro, Spanish for "treasure." He was a beautiful black dog with tan socks, and Tito and I shared in the responsibilities of caring for him, after begging our father to let us keep him. Tito fed him and I shoveled his shit. Nothing could separate us.

But our neighbors complained and threatened police intervention. Our father took Tesoro away to stay with an uncle who lived on a ranch, where he would be happy on the farm, my father promised. He would be free to roam the ranch and the surrounding apple orchards. But, at the farm, they imprisoned him, kept him on a leash, tortured him into becoming a worthy guard dog. Until one day

Tesoro attacked one of the farm goats and acquired another taste for blood.

Farm life changed him as it did me.

When I saw Tesoro on the farm, I reached for my beloved dog's head, despite his barking. Maybe, just maybe, if I touched him again, he'd remember the good times. He'd remember me. His ribs protruded. This dog who bit into my lip was not the dog I knew for years, the dog who protected me from bullies, and raced to embrace Tito and me. Either he mistook me for someone else—another torturer who would poke him with a stick until he turned mean—or he knew exactly who I was, and took this opportunity to lash out in anger at me, for abandoning him to this harsh life where no one loved him or fed him properly.

When Tesoro went after another goat, he was shot and buried there on the ranch, where like all other slaughtered life his blood seeped into the soil that enrich our orchards and vineyards.

✦

I think about Tesoro's affection on the run, which allows me to explore what physical touch means to me. In the jungles, for instance, I experience the touch of rain—a rain unlike what I experienced at home. A kind of rain that almost brings on a fever. I had lost touch with the world around me, and it would be through my touch of animals, people, and the land that I would move toward recovery.

27

The Rebirth of Story

August 12. Mazatlán, Sinaloa. Roughly 4,100 tangled miles.

It's another hot day and we're on a sweaty run through the congested streets near the beach town of Mazatlán. There's a fire within me from forcing down jalapeños to ease my worry of stomach infection. Cheeto and I slip through the chaos like professional athletes. Passersby turn their heads toward us in silence.

"Why don't people say hello to us?" Cheeto asks me between breaths.

"Maybe because we look like we're in a hurry?" I tell him. "And because we smell."

Something catches his eye. "Ever had La Michoacana?" he asks.

"No," I say.

He gives me a look of shock. "Come with me!" He veers off course.

I follow him into a shop selling ice cream. In line, we talk.

Cheeto was brought into the U.S. from Mexico when he was two or three years old, to join his father who was already working in the U.S. "At the border, it hit me," Cheeto says. "I was coming back to another nation that I knew." Cheeto places coins on the counter, asks me what flavor, and receives two *helados*. We peel the wrappers, uncovering coconut and strawberry, and run out of the store—staffs in one hand, *helado* in another.

✦

We take a day of rest in Mazatlán, Sinaloa, in a vacant lobby of a hotel rumored to belong to drug cartels. It is said that laundered money is what built these cities. We clean out the vans, bringing order to our corner of an orderless world. We are engaged in familiar tasks—tending to our battered legs, breathing in the salty ions of the coast, playing music—when Pacquiao calls a meeting.

"Everyone please gather around," Pacquiao says. His face is stern. "Today I received an email from someone in Washington State." He looks around, into the eyes of every runner. I know it's about me. "The email states that we could face legal action on the grounds that we are denying runners water."

My heart stops. Earlier on the run, I stopped in an Internet café and emailed a professor of mine about Trigger's withholding water from us.

"Whoever sent this email, please come forward," Pacquiao says.

No one does. For a long while there's silence. Pacquiao gives me the chance to come forward, but I don't. This is not the time to confront Trigger, I think to myself.

"Well, I expect that whoever sent this information out will fix it," Pacquiao says. "And I mean soon."

At the earliest opportunity, I send an email informing my professor that things are now much better, when, in fact, they are not. My days and nights are spent around Trigger. Pacquiao can guarantee me no safety.

28

Nayarit

The rains hit heavily for several days, slapping against us as we push forward through the green hills around us. The towns we pass through blur into each other. Many of us are now running with one hand on a feathered staff and the other against a riotous stomach. Infections are common, but I am not afflicted, not yet. The jalapeños at work, maybe. Still, darting into the bushes has become common practice, with dehydration and nutrient loss ever-present risks. But we run it out, feeling that the harder we run, the quicker we'll cleanse our systems of sickness.

"We're becoming like animals," Mazat says admiringly, while we run together. "Almost capable of distinguishing the different kinds of rain like animals do." The manner in which the rain strikes, strums, and plucks at our skins, as if our bodies were like the chords of an instrument.

✦

For closing Circle, while Tlaloc and Trigger prepare their musical instruments, Zyanya Lonewolf asks me to do something: "Stand up." I do.

"Now reach your hands as high as possible," like touching a ceiling, Zyanya Lonewolf explains. "That there is the spirit world. That's how close it is." Tlaloc and Trigger sing in the Nahuatl Indigenous language a song dedicated to Tonantzin. Zyanya Lonewolf, who has been learning songs with Trigger, tells me that the song is dedicated to an "Aztec goddess."

"What do you think they are singing about?" I ask Zyanya Lonewolf for more detail.

"Something about how we're pitiful humans on earth just trying to find our place on the land." The special place that's located between earth and sky and that can be touched by reaching your hands high, she says.

After the conch had passed through many hands in Circle, Mazat had expressed frustrations with the northern Chicanx runners—us, people who came into Mexico with an attitude, energy, air of prestige that clashed with the local runners of Mexico.

"Here in the south, traditions and ceremony are very land-specific and those laws must be respected," he says. In his view, PDJ imposed ceremonial protocols different from those of locals, widening the cultural divide between the northern runners of the U.S. and Canada, and people in Mexico. "I don't know about you guys, but down here in Mexico, we are always in ceremony. All of our lives we've been in ceremony."

This discussion comes about after lightning had struck and a local runner interpreted it with foreboding—claiming it was a sign that the runners were running incorrectly and that we were mishandling the feathered staffs. Mazat made demands, but Pacquiao wouldn't have any of it. "We run in all weather. The running doesn't stop," he said. Mazat—a man proud of his people's ways and heritage—felt responsible for his people and the few Sonoran runners permitted to join the vans in Mexico. It became yet another bitter dispute lasting into the late hours.

"The Mexican vision seems to be different from the Chicano version," Mazat remarked in Spanish about the organization of the run, while Cheeto interpreted in English for the others. "Running and imposing our ways on communities does not comply with the mandates of the run," he continues, drawing smoke from his pipe. The hours are long, runners fidget, and I massage the pain stabbing my knees. "There are people with a superior mentality here, who don't run, even pretend to be sick," he says. He tells about how runners don't properly share things with one another—basic items donated by the communities, food, musical instruments. About feeling rejected sometimes by the "English speakers of the north," he says. Around the camp are people's wet clothes, wrung socks. "We make promises to the communities. The run should not be led with arrogance."

✦

Chula Pepper voices another pressing concern. Sexism on the run.

She reminds us of the "Woman Warrior" song. How as the song went through the U.S., it changed, taking on the spirit of the different places, absorbing the words and strength of women who wanted change. But she was upset, she said. "It's frustrating to be told that you can't walk in front of the drum because you'll curse the drummer," she said. There was a lot of superstition around women on their period. "I'm upset at certain rules around the drums. That if we're on our moon or wear certain clothing, that it's disrespectful in a lot communities." The implied assumption is that if you are uncovered in any way, you're distracting men and taking their strength from running. Chula Pepper had the support of most runners.

"The 'Woman Warrior' song is *our* song," she asserts. "We're the strong ones. It's our song to teach and empower other women with."

✦

For a time the meeting improves relationships between runners. We give it our best to be civil. But exhaustion and short fuses pull us back apart, back into old patterns of mere survival. Running when we barely walk. Staying awake when we barely can sleep.

29

Mangoes

Several miles southwest of Nayarit, Mexico, a desert village wakens to cool air. The blooming sun exposes me squatted behind a rock on the edge of camp, beside the shade of a large shrub, swatting away at flies materializing out of my ass. I wipe then sit on a rock to contemplate the contours of Nayarit—an arid land in southwest Mexico situated along the Pacific coast. My stomach grumbles. I soak in a new day.

A collective silhouette of village kids comes over the hills. Baskets of laundry rest on their heads. Buckets swing from their hands. They dip into the black hills to collect water and wash clothes. One of the boys walks toward me. After a moment, he points to the bag of dried fruit beside me and gestures with his hand to his mouth. I hand it to him, he kisses me on the shoulder, and walks away.

✦

The run is increasingly sluggish, food supply is low, and some of us have gaunt looks to our faces. We are getting desperate. The salmon jerky from Alaska has long run out. Canned foods are low. Villagers offer what little they can to us. The run is purging us on many levels, but without the proper nourishment, I know I cannot sustain running for much longer. My knees continue to throb, and I continue to ignore them.

Later, when the van drives by a mango grove, Andrec brakes. Struck by the same idea, Cheeto, Andrec, and I devise a way to collect mangos. Rather than deplete local families of their food, Cheeto, Andrec, and I take to a single tree. We pick unripe mangoes, quickly tossing them down to Cheeto, and into the van.

We eat unripe mangoes for nearly a week, it seems, snapping crunchy fruit into our mouths like apples. We pay the consequences: diarrheal detours.

Still, the run goes on and the mangoes sustain us. We are only small pieces of personality pushing forward toward better versions of ourselves as best as we can. We are dirty, smelly, and we often frustrate one another. Complaints range from minor ones, like me discovering that Trigger is giving me more miles to cover, to serious ones relating to safety.

The roads are not roads at all in this part of Mexico. Only wrinkles and gashes in the earth hacked out by a fury of weather and the migration of animals and villagers. Our van trembles onward until we stop and set up camp. I duck into the shrubbery and set up my tent. The hard, dry soil crunches beneath my feet. Short outgrowths of grass scruff my knees. Thorny branches prod my sleeves. A grasshopper is awash in a river of ants. A kestrel kneads its talons into a rodent. My mind bites greedily into Mexico, tracking my moves forward, and forcing me to see things in a new way. A spider repairs its web. Near it, bent grass. Fur is snagged to small twigs. Signs of a disturbance. A hoof that has cut through the orb of a web. I squat and see fresh scat. The light shifts and for a moment everything makes sense to me. My ears ring with adrenaline.

I sit down beside my tent. Suddenly, a cool shiver fills me. Death, I realize, takes a thousand forms. I close my eyes until it all goes away.

What am I doing with my life?

30

Santo Coyote

Guadalajara, México. Roughly 4,500 miles from Prince George, British Columbia, Canada, where I started.

Chula Pepper lifts her head from the side of the street, where she's been vomiting. Passersby look almost judgingly at her. They seem to know even before she does that she is pregnant.

We runners go inside the five-star Santo Coyote Restaurant—an adobe structure like that of the Flintstones', carrying a mixed atmosphere of New Mexican mysticism, Sioux and Navajo culture. The place is almost cartoonish, housing collectors' items like peace pipes, statues, animal fur, and high-end tequila. Totem poles and palm trees adorned with dream catchers stand in a lush garden. Wicker lanterns hang like glowing beehives over our dinner tables. Chiseled into the walls are Egyptian and Hindu figures, tribal chieftains, and framed images of Catholic saints. A playland of commercialized culture.

Pacquiao, a mentor to Chula Pepper, sits privately with her to discuss next steps.

From Santo Coyote, we run sixty miles through streets vibrant with cafés, art galleries, and scented with orchid, ceiba, and *tabachín del monte* flowers that are bursting over walls like cotton candy forgotten there by children. It is the expat town of Ajijic in Lake Chapala in the state of Jalisco. Here we are received by local artists. We set down our feathered staffs after closing Circle. Some of us take a walk to the pier that overlooks the great Lake Chapala, a lake slowly choked off by the growth of lotus and green foliage. On its banks are swarms of herons. An occasional water snake slithers into the tangle of vegetation. Cheeto, Andrec, Zyanya Lonewolf, and I stroll through the outdoor markets, inspect merchandise, appreciate some art, and buy water and snacks.

We engage in an effort to see with new eyes—with our feet—in a movement that is something like friction and capturing our feelings of isolation, displacement, even exile.

When we return to the café where we will sleep, Chula Pepper announces to the group her departure from the run. She is leaving to let her body prepare for motherhood. She wants to raise her baby alone, because, she says, "I do not want my kid to have a false sense of a father figure."

What an enchanting place, Lake Chapala, to conclude the run, I think to myself.

31

Hardware Store

My father is always occupied in work, and when he pauses he teaches me his work of landscaping, home repair, and basic construction. Between the orchards, we often visited the hardware store together after hauling some trash or other from worksites to the dump in nearby Terrace Heights.

The thing that always hit me most about the store was the smell. Mulch and plywood. A smell to contrast that of the orchards. I followed him through the aisles, learning his trade at an early age, observing him sift his fingers over things like boxes of nails and fasteners, feeling, reading, and inspecting his way around. It was as if he was envisioning in his mind the things he would repair or construct without much understanding of the English language. The door, window frame, a fence, or rooftop he would install or repair.

He would point and say things like, "Find me a two and

a half," and I would jump at the opportunity to help him, copying the same motions as his, painting my fingers over nail boxes, inspecting and absorbing the magic not only of the place, but of my father's tracks. I knew even then, deep in my heart, that when my father passes, I can become reacquainted with him in places such as these hardware stores.

He inspects the lumber boards, evaluates their cut, reads their grain to determine integrity. "Place them in the cart," he tells me.

I do so proudly, laying the wood, no matter that splinters lodge in my fingers.

In another area, there are doors on display on hinges. Before leaving the store, I quickly turn them like pages, pretend to walk through them into a different world.

32

Weaving Words

August 30. Morelia, Michoacán.

My knees immobilize me inside the bustling baroque city of Morelia, Michoacán, roughly 310 miles north of my father's hometown of La Cruz de Campos. Street vendors, cobblestone streets, grand architecture, folkloric festivals, verdant plazas, tropical gardens, and water fountains abound in all directions here in Morelia. Here, the run takes a rest among the locals in one of the central gardens where large plumes of copal smoke smudge the air. A group of spinning *danzantes* clears a path like whirls of air and magnetize a crowd. I sit this one out on a bench, in pain, too stubborn to call it quits. Families and children gather around, corn on the cob, chips, and candy in their hands.

It is on this day that I am taken to the Morelia hospital. Large liquid pockets have formed around my knees, and they are choking off circulation to my knees. If I don't quit,

I could suffer permanent damage to my knees, the doctor tells me.

"Why are you running?" the doctor asks me.

"*Corro por mi familia.*" For my family, I tell him.

He looks at me. I'm prescribed painkillers and sent on my way.

While the runners go away to tackle steep hillsides in Pátzcuaro, I am comfortably housed and fed in the city, treated in a candlelit room in a place of worship where alternative-medical practitioners drain my swollen knees with needles. I learn that some of them hold high positions of influence in the city, that they are lawyers, businessmen, artists.

One of these men is Helvio, a political refugee, writer, and philosopher from Uruguay. He invites me to rest in his home—partly converted into a bookstore. He spends his days among corridors of bookshelves, taking breaks to smoke his pipe on a chair on the sidewalk.

Helvio and I speak about the ache of exile, feelings of isolation, and what it might mean to stand up for what one believes.

"Writing can be a medium for spiritual awareness, social justice," he says. "Change can be activated in a society by way of story."

He tells me that because of his refusal to keep quiet, his stories, activism, he was ousted from the only home he ever knew: Uruguay.

"If you create words and repeat them enough, they can

elicit change." He knocks his pipe against his foot and reloads it with tobacco. "Our words," he says, "must be hurled with precision."

For me, the language of PDJ has been in our feet. Like language, running creates us and holds us accountable to the world around us—committing our own bodies to every inch of earth across our North American journey.

Every time a person opens their mouth, that person re-creates himself. Running invites us to reimagine our future—where running is used to reestablish unity with others. This is why running stories are timeless. We are what we imagine, according to the Kiowa author N. Scott Momaday. And if we imagine a better future, and speak it with words and the soles of our feet, we just might see it come to fruition.

33

The Flying Men of Teotihuacán

The PDJ run also traces the origin story of the Aztecs—an ancient people who left their mythical homeland of Aztlán (located somewhere in northwest Mexico) after the revelation of a prophecy, in pursuit of a new place to settle. They embarked on a two-hundred-year journey, wandering and establishing communities along the way, into Lake Chapala in Jalisco, Pátzcuaro in Michoacán, and many others, until finally anchoring themselves in the place where the prophecy was said to come to life—an eagle that perched itself on a cactus tearing its talons into a snake. It is now the emblem on the Mexican flag. Where the Aztecs founded their capital of Tenochtitlán stands on present-day Mexico City. In their many years of wandering, they adapted their name to Mexica, which gave rise to the name Mexico.

Mexico City is a monster. Six-, seven-, eight-lane traffic.

A free-for-all driving atmosphere where pedestrians do not have the right of way. The traffic lights turn red and homeless children scramble out from under bridges with water bottles and dirty rags in hand. They make the rounds through traffic and encircle vehicles, our van included. Sickly children step onto the front tires and clean the windows.

I observe one boy in particular as he wipes our van's windows with a rag. His eyes are on me. Here we are. Two Latino extremes. Me, inside, the privileged traveler. He, outside. Coins are handed over, and the children retreat when the flow of traffic resumes. This reality is hard to get used to.

When we run, hopping onto edges, skirting large vehicles, trying not to get swept into the stream of cars, I hold my staff up high, hoping to signal cars behind me of my presence. We enter underpasses at our own peril, sucking in thick plumes of diesel fumes, and dodging pedestrian traffic like soccer players. I blow black snot rockets from all the smog. It's a miracle that some of us find our markers at all. This is the chaos that we try to navigate.

Again and again, runners are dropped off at intervals while another van tries desperately to relocate us for pickup. The task of standing out in a crowd is difficult. But we do our best. At times, we move faster than the vans held up in traffic. Unable to wait for pickup sometimes, we take on more miles, run and run until we cannot go any longer, until the vans come for us.

✦

Later, the staffs are set onto blankets on the ancient grounds near the Templo Mayor, the epicenter of everything Mexican. Here also is Mexico's presidential palace. Vendors bustle with activity in the Zócalo—an island of concrete. I wander off during Ceremony toward the Metropolitan Cathedral. It's askew and sinking due to the soft soil. A soil that will one day consume us all.

I then wander into an old bookstore, peruse the Spanish books, buy a newspaper and read it in one of the *portales* on a gritty corner overlooking the Zócalo. I buy a black coffee. It feels good to be seated among normal people, to feel part of society again, despite the glances.

Crow investigates a commotion happening between Tlaloc and a woman who surprise-visited him in Mexico City. She's yelling at him, striking and slapping him, then chasing him through the streets while he ducks for cover. Later, Tlaloc approaches Crow while she orders tacos from a street vendor to tell her that he loves only her.

"But wasn't that your girlfriend?" she asks, having heard from the other runners.

"No. Not anymore," he answers her. "I just broke up with her."

✦

At a ceremonial gathering at the ruins of Teotihuacán, northeast of Mexico City, a group of Indigenous men, *voladores* of the Totonac Nation, climb a hundred-foot pole where they then tie themselves to ropes and swing down in circular motion like buzzards over prey. It is an ancient ceremonial practice. Four men swinging in the sky outstretch their arms like many crucified Christs. A fifth man sits at the apex and plays a flute. I cannot imagine the feeling. When the men finally reach bottom, they extend the rope to us. One of them is an elderly man, in his seventies. I decline the invitation.

Something about the flight of these men reminds me of a day when I was a child, and my uncle, Gonzalo, my father's brother, was visiting. I noticed a large crow perched on the low part of a tree in an orchard in Yakima. Gonzalo, seated in the car next to me, encouraged me to grab it despite my father's warnings that the bird was sick and dying. But Gonzalo was older. He nudged me. I got out of the car, stepped up into the tree and reached for the crow. It did not resist. I spent the rest of the day playing with my new friend. I walked everywhere with the crow perched on my arm, introducing it to the orchard grounds. I combed the grass for worms and tried feeding it. But it ate very little. I picked and bit parts of apples and tried feeding it this way. No appetite. As the day progressed, I tried encouraging it to fly, but it wouldn't. It lacked the will to fly. When the workday came to an end and the men packed into the car again, I perched the crow onto my wrist and walked with it to the car.

"Noé. Let it go," my dad commanded.

Gonzalo agreed. "It wants to die. Let it die in the trees, where it belongs."

I knew at the time that they were right, but didn't want to believe that my bird was dying. Maybe it could be saved, if just given the chance. I left it on a branch and walked back to the car. It never settled right with me, this idea that things can want to die.

✦

This evening, Trigger and Tlaloc call for a vote to eliminate a few runners, including me, from the run. Everyone is tense.

"We believe there are runners here not honoring the ways of our ancestors. They consume our food, take up space, and are unwilling to run the mileage," Trigger begins. "They don't honor the ways of the run."

"It's a hard truth to face: The run is not for everyone. We hang on longer than we should. We don't want to go home when we should. But it's a difficult choice for everyone. These runners stay and suck the spirit out of the run," Tlaloc adds.

Cheeto, Andrec, myself, and others are named. We defend one another. I disclose all that Trigger has done wrong. I call him out on his flaws, his abuse of power, how he contaminates the run with gang philosophy, and is someone who cannot be trusted. In solidarity, Cheeto brings attention to Tlaloc's own acts. Circle quickly spirals into a heated shouting match between runners, who hold nothing back.

Suddenly, to everyone's surprise, Zyanya Lonewolf announces her resignation from the run. The problems on the run have reached new heights, she says, and she does not want to bear the weight any longer. Circle adjourns, and later in the evening, Trigger and Tlaloc follow me back to the van when I'm alone. They close the van door, trapping me inside.

In the face of their threats to watch my back, I fear even more for my safety.

Later that evening, I climb up the Sun Pyramid, and sit overlooking the sunset. I reflect on what was said to me. The power of their words has cut me open, and I am forced to confront what I've have known all along—that I am living in an illusion and that my time on the run is soon coming to an end.

34

Descending Eagle

We run to the burial ground of the last Aztec emperor, Cuauhtémoc ("Descending Eagle"), in Santa Maria de la Asunción Church overlooking the beautiful town of Ixcateopan, in Guerrero. Like many Mexican towns, the place is fashioned in the colonial style of its Spanish conquerors, laid with cobblestone roads, white adobe structures, and red-tiled roofs extending from here to the neighboring silver-mining town of Taxco.

We settle inside the church to have Ceremony around a glass ossuary of the Aztec emperor. The bones are said to have been recovered from under the church—one of the many tactics of psychological warfare employed by the Spanish *conquistadores* to erase any memory of Indigenous revolt was by building churches over sacred grounds.

"His people never gave up searching," Cheeto tells me. In

many ways the Mexican people still search for him. "They never believed that he had abandoned them."

We reflect on what Pacquiao had said about how there's a long history of oppression, a history that often feels like it has seeped into the land, and how part of the work of running is to be able to uncover that and break that up. So that "violence doesn't get incorporated any further into our cultures, getting passed down like a hereditary gene," Pacquiao said.

"We're all responsible for taking care of one another," Cheeto adds. "Healing through culture, healing in a way that is grounded in identity."

"That's the ceremony of running," Andrec concludes.

35

Oaxaca

The harsh elements appear to relent roughly 5,600 miles from Prince George, B.C., Canada, in the state of Oaxaca where our run breezes along the coastline. The air is sweet and it whips our sweat from us. Our stay is fairly short in this state, and we take resting points along the Pacific Ocean. One such stop is under straw ramada.

It's customary to gather for Circle after a run, before laying the staffs to rest. On this particular day the gathering of people is large. We're into our third hour of Circle. Many of us runners are shifting our weight, shaking the pain throbbing in our knees, and salivating over the abundance of food getting cold on a nearby table that the community has set with beans, rice, tortillas, and tamales. It is brutal to watch the food get cold.

Like a household of siblings, we eye the food we'll get to

first. I eye the tamales, imagining the flavors of my mom's home cooking.

"Look at those frijolitos." Cheeto leans toward me, as desperate to savor the food as I am. "Are those chicharrones?"

Despite the fairly consistent rhythm of eating twice a day, before and after the run, we still often fight hunger, what feels like kicks to the stomach and head. It causes us lightheadedness, grumpiness. Fatigue. Division. We become ravenous animals with short fuses. But this, some say, is the warrior way, and to people like Trigger, some of us are not suffering enough. "The ceremony of Sun Dance is in pain," he often says.

We dash to the table after Closing Ceremony, pack our plates, and indulge in food until we get stomachaches. In moments like these, the tongue becomes hyperaware of taste, savoring everything as if for the first time. The fatty oils are especially fatty, it seems, after a long run. The salts especially salty.

After filling our bellies, some of us rest on hammocks under the ramada, others plop straight onto the sand itself. This part of the coast seems unperturbed by tourists or even locals. Silence under an ocean wind. The best kind. The water is shallow, low tide, and for several hundred feet, Cheeto, Andrec, Chenoa, Refugio, and I walk into the horizon toward a red sun. We dip ourselves into the temperate waters, nourishing ourselves with the minerals. A single raft is moored on the sand, wedged between water and soil. It rocks over the nudging water like a baby's crib.

I dip my fingers into this holy water and think about my father when he too squatted as a boy over the edge of the Pacific Ocean, coming from La Cruz de Campos, Michoacán, to cast iguanas into the water and hunt for crabs. When he tracked the edge for turtle eggs while his stomach burned with hunger. A lot has happened since that time. My father has come a long way, and now it is my duty to go farther. And the kids after me, even farther. I step into these waters as if to cast my own body into its whole memory of life and death. As if to let the water know whose son I am. To ask it to release us of any ill will, for any past wrongs our family may have inflicted onto the cosmos, and to let us grow. Here, I ask the water for forgiveness. To wash me of the pain passed down from father to father to son to brother.

36

Zapatistas: Rebel Country

We plunge farther into new lands—the state of Chiapas, Tuxtla Gutiérrez, the autonomous Zapatista villages of Oventic, then Acteal, and the Agua Azul waterfall deep in the Lacandon Jungle, a green muscle flexing across Honduras and Guatemala.

It is an ink wash of a world here in rainy Chiapas where we traverse steep highlands with heavy feet, moving about the clouds as if in some dream world that smells of firewood. Roads coil around remote Mayan villages that appear and disappear in the fog like ghost towns. The silhouettes of women hunching over the land can be seen in the clouds, working the land, and carrying bundles of firewood on their backs. I run, parting the mist with my body, observing these lands—a state with the highest poverty rate in Mexico.

From these harsh lands erupted a movement that caught the world's attention in 1994. The Mayan people of these lands took up arms and seized towns across Chiapas, fed up with generations of evictions, encroachments on their land, and mass displacement. Leading them was a figure who emerged on horseback as if from the mist of the Lacandon Jungle. A man in a ski mask, smoking a pipe, who went by the *nom de guerre* of Subcomandante Marcos. "El Sub" for short. Thousands of Indigenous people in ski masks declared war on the Mexican government as part of the Ejército Zapatista de Liberación Nacional (EZLN). The Zapatista Army of National Liberation.

El Sub was said to wear two watches—one to track society's time and another to track Indigenous time. "The movement will stop only when the two watches become in sync," he will say in an interview with reporter Carlos Loret de Mola of Primero Noticias de Televisa Chapultepec, on May 9, 2006. "When society finally understands our place as Indigenous villages. Only then will there be a single time. United."

We enter the autonomous town of Oventic, which El Sub helped protect under the orders of the Mayan tribal council of Chiapas. These autonomous villages are collectively referred to as *los Caracoles*. "Snails," in English, because they are defensive by nature and are content to take their time. Their spiraling shell pattern symbolizes an ideology that will radiate across the globe. Pacquiao approaches the gates, communicates our intentions to one of the ski-masked commanders, and undergoes a thorough inspection. They review his papers, make the necessary inquiries, then wave the vans inside, onto their lands. We pass a sign reading, YOU ARE NOW IN REBEL ZAPATISTA TERRITORY. HERE, THE PEOPLE COMMAND AND THE GOVERNMENT OBEYS.

✦

We enter into a wooden lodge—its facade is painted with a large mural of Emiliano Zapata. Above it, the words: SNAIL MU'KTA TZOB'ONBAIL. We enter the lodge. There's a stage, a large Mexican flag, and a music band. Surrounding us in a circle are more men and women in masks. Tacked to the walls are papers with lists of international organizations in support of the Zapatista cause. Lines of spotted lights—like Christmas ornaments, set the mood for a fiesta. Despite our exhaustion, I watch the runners dance in celebration.

The melancholic vocals of Indigenous artists in ski masks resound against this pine lodge and earth floor, while I sit and watch my colleagues. What I feel is love. I watch my friends with warmth, every one of them, proud to call them my family. I watch them, us, in our imperfections, in our passion to be better, commitment to be present for others over ourselves. Refugio's acceptance that every person is good. Cheeto's unrestrained humor. Chenoa with a heart for singing twice the size of anybody else's. Andrec's unwavering balance and centeredness. Pacquiao, who in many ways has to carry the great load of us—leading us into uncharted territory, counting on us to persevere. Even Tlaloc's and Trigger's strict regimens of self-discovery. Every one of them pushed me to build the muscle to confront my problems. Here, I make my decision to call it quits on the run. But only once we are in Guatemala. I let Cheeto know.

"What are you going to do?" he asks.

"I don't really know," I tell him. "But whatever I do, I'll have to do it soon." I grip my knees. "I'm not fully in it anymore."

"PDJ can do that. It can pull you in another direction. Into another river. If home's where you need to be, it's where you need to be, amigo." He puts his hand on my shoulder.

I struggle to stand up and I join the line of dancers. For a moment I try to ride the beauty of the Chiapas people engaged in the beautiful act of community. I absorb this like a sponge, to last me the rest of my life.

✦

The following morning, ski-masked men, women, and children meet us in a field of corn. They have a saying here, Andrec tells me. "We cover our faces so that you can finally see us." They lead us into their community. At one point, women in straw hats and ponytails smudge us—each of us still holding our staffs. But not Tlaloc, who has torn a green cornstalk from one of his runs and carries it proudly to "help heal the harvest," he tells the villagers who thank him. "Corn represents life. We owe her our souls." This is Tlaloc as a runner, improvising to the beats of his surroundings. Tlaloc as a nonrunner, well, part of me still admires him, but things have grown worse between him and me. It is as if running can no longer suppress the people we really are inside. Hungry, exhausted, and impatient, we resort to old habits, take our frustrations out on one another. Blame failures on everyone but ourselves, myself included. Still, we continue forward, nourishing ourselves with the spirit of these lands as best we can.

37

Acteal

Cheeto, Andrec, and I enter an *abarrotes* convenience store. My mission is only one: to pack as much sugar into my body as possible. On the curbside of this small village, I sit and dump cupcakes and beverage packages around me. One by one I peel them open, intent on replenishing with junk food the nourishment I have lost. Cheeto and Andrec do as I do. We're like kids. It's a treat to myself, dammit. I've earned this.

"When exactly will you be leaving us, Noé?" Andrec asks me.

"Soon. Very soon." I feel guilt for leaving them behind. I begin to feel the real fear of Tlaloc's promise to make me pay. "Sorry I no longer have it in me."

"Have you told Pacquiao?" they ask.

I have told Pacquiao how ashamed I am of leaving the

team. For failing to care for my legs properly. I just want to make it across all of Mexico. As soon as we reach the Guatemalan border, I will find a bus to take me to the nearest airport.

The three of us pack the final sugary snacks into our systems and sit back, a kind of joy blazing in us.

✦

Near the region of San Cristóbal de las Casas, Chiapas, in a region scarred by deep valleys, steep mountains, and dark muddy ravines, a constant drizzle makes the streets glisten and moistens my face. A ways away into my run, I come upon three smiling kids. Two are on a bike, a brother and a sister—she in a muddied dress, her brother in a Spider-Man shirt. Their friend is in a patterned wool sweater and walks beside them.

We play off of each other's energies, each picking up the pace until we're in a full-fledged race. Their laughter melts my heart. I cheat and set off into the grass. They bring out the kid in me again, and I dash over the soft soil and suck in the pine-flavored air around me. The burst of energy rejuvenates me, and I think of the Yakima Valley—the river and hills. Of my family. The children know these lands—every wrinkle of earth and hair of grass—better than I do. They know happiness better than I do. I run even harder, all to make them laugh when suddenly my knees are gripped by an excruciating torture, like knives twisting into them.

There I sit, feeling like a failure, bracing the flesh of my legs. I go no farther.

This, I think, is where it all ends for me.

The van comes for me later in the day and takes me to camp. With no hospitals anywhere nearby, I am instead visited that evening by a local medicine man. He shoves peyote into my mouth and gestures to me to swallow. He smudges me with eagle feathers, incense, and chants.

We conclude our trip through Chiapas by running to the turquoise waters of the Agua Azul waterfalls before leaving for the Palenque ruins. There, we trace the blue water and dip ourselves in it—yet again letting the land become acquainted with the taste of us. Before leaving for the Palenque ruins, I dip my feet into the river bubbling with the flavors of the jungle, like tea, and I let all my problems slip away into the water like sediment. My final run approaches.

38

Guatemala

Roughly 6,300 miles. On the floor of an abandoned church near a remote village south of the Zaculeu ruins, I wake from a bad dream to the sound of howling street dogs. Enveloping us is the smell of must and sage. My bandaged legs pulse and oppress me. The moment has arrived for me to leave the run. While everyone is still asleep, I gather my belongings, open my 1,600-page dictionary to confirm the little money I hid for a return flight home is still there, and walk into the foggy night.

I look around at the empty cobblestone streets. Cheeto grabs my arm. "You take care, homie."

He goes back inside.

Packs of stray dogs canvass the streets, hurrying as if to some secret meal. They disappear like ghosts. I walk to a bus stop across town, feeling sad that I will not be able to finish the run. Despite my knees' protests, I post myself against an adobe wall and stand against the mist as it butters past me, not knowing if there really is a bus. The bus departs once a day, a villager told me the day before. Finally, with the rising sun, a brightly colored bus arrives. After I board, it drives noisily through pine forest and foggy open country, toward Guatemala City.

While I jump into an airplane for home, to rest and heal, the other runners, I imagine, finally gather in jubilation at the opposite ends of the Bridge of the Americas in Panama. There, Crow unwraps the Warrior Flag held in her hand. Holding on when others couldn't, gripping that flag as hard as if it were an extension of everything meaningful in her life. When the time comes, she and others launch themselves forward toward the finish line, Crow waving the flag against the wind.

The main feathered staff has gained the weight of so many feathers that a flare of wind threatens to lift the runner holding the staff aloft into the heavens. It has absorbed a world of stories since its inception in Chickaloon Village, Alaska, where it only had three: the eagle, macaw, and condor feathers.

✦

The end of the run, I hear later, does not feel like an uncomplicated victory. Even in the comfort of a hotel, Cheeto and other runners worry about their families. Mazat sits and smokes outside on the steps of a hotel in Panama without a dollar to his name, dwelling over how he'll return home. Meanwhile, Pacquiao sits hunched inside his car, beaten down by disappointment. Word reached Gustavo—his mentor back home—about his failure to organize better. The infighting, the chaos. Pacquiao feels unappreciated and unacknowledged. A sickness would consume his body for months and he would vow never to lead PDJ again.

✦

For everyone, the world that we had put on pause was beginning to move again.

FREE

39

Old Orchard

For months after the run, I rest, at home among my people in Yakima. I rest on the couch by day, and sleep on the floor of my bedroom at night, unable to adjust to the comforts of a bed and pillow. Although my knees are finally free of bandages, my spirit continues to heal still enwrapped in the dream that is PDJ. I kick and throb in my sleep. Still running.

Months later, when my legs feel strong again, I revisit the old apple orchard of my childhood. I take my mother's car and drive toward the familiar west. I grow excited at the thought of becoming reacquainted with my relatives that are the land and the trees. I come to the crest of a hill, turn into the property and—

The apple trees have been leveled. Not a single root around. None of the branches left that had supported my weight when I had scaled them. Timidly, I knock on the front door of the adjoining house to ask for permission to wander the premises. A young boy answers the door with one eye showing through the slit. It's okay, he tells me.

I walk over the old land as a mature person now, on a land no longer rippled like ribs of a human by the wheels of tractors, thinking back to when I was a child, when I pummeled the dry, compact earth with the force of a young boy believing himself a man, wielding a shovel against the gusts of wind, dressed in the baggy clothes of my father, which I sometimes liked to borrow. When I leaned with one foot on the shovel, arms on the handle, to observe my father in the distance manning a diesel tractor. I know now that every bit of earth contains the sacredness of another person's existence.

Aided by a foundation of peace, dignity, and self-love, I return to the adventures of college several months later. This time, I achieve degrees in philosophy and creative writing from Whitman and Emerson Colleges. In between those two schools, I complete a fellowship at Princeton University's Woodrow Wilson School of Public and International Affairs, and study conflict analysis, peacemaking, and conflict resolution at American University in D.C. I commit to these intellectual pursuits like someone making up for lost time and still restless and pushing myself forward, trying to figure things out. I delve into grassroots work and study U.S. drug policy, military aid, and human-rights issues in Colombia inside the jungles of Putumayo. I meet with parliamentary figures of Northern Ireland and lead an art delegation to Mexico, soaking in as much of the world as I can and searching for that "better" version of myself. I teach youth and work inside food banks, helping homeless and substance-abuse populations. I seek elsewhere the spiritual and philosophical truths that running provided me. But within myself I believe that these truths can be achieved without a college education. The world tells me that achievement has to look one way, but I struggle with that.

In Seattle, for a time, I venture into dishwashing. My face drips in the hot mist of towering dishes as I hose and feed them through a commercial dishwasher. In ninety-second intervals, steam emerges from the machine in suffocating plumes that redden my face. In the back, cutting boards chatter under the cutlery as potatoes and tomatoes are diced, and oysters are peeled and parted. Balls of dough slap onto flour beds. Hands shape them into braids. Paper ticket orders queue from a machine like sausage links over chef José's blazing pans: shepherd's pie, soup, oysters. José's forehead gleams as he prepares and garnishes plates. With rag in hand, he slams shut a red-hot oven door and curses through his teeth, "I need oysters, potatoes, limes, *rapido*." I collect and wash oysters. With a knife, I jab at the stubborn crustacean mouths inches over my palm. There's never time to put on gloves. When the chef calls for potatoes, I hobble back with a fifty-pound orange net of large potatoes, wash four dozen, and shave long brown skins from them. Peeled potatoes slip from my hand into a splashing bucket of water, and I place the load at José's feet. "Here are the potatoes and oysters, boss."

As the dinner wave calms, and the fall evening sun sets over the drizzle outside, I step from the noise into a nook in the narrow hallway used for breaks, where a single chair and table glow under yellow lighting. Others are already resting there. I sit on the floor, my back against the wall, and pull out a paperback to read.

The kitchen's double doors open. "What are you all doing sitting around? Hell. Look at this," Old Lady Kelly—the tireless restaurant owner—tosses empty boxes from random shelves. "Break these boxes!"

Her eyes fix on me sitting in the corner. "Come here," she says, and I get up and follow. "Take this bucket and fill it with Clorox. Here—wipe this table down—no, not like that—why the hell did you do that? Bring that trash bin here—quickly—use this."

I clean over and under the baking table with old rags drenched in Clorox as Mrs. Kelly storms around the kitchen. I keep myself moving, wringing Clorox rags, grabbing brooms, breaking boxes, removing dirty towels, nesting buckets, and often responding with downcast eyes: "Yes, ma'am," and, "Right away."

In the restroom, the cleaning chemicals burn my nostrils as I scrub the walls of the bathrooms, the urinals, and get in behind the toilets. My shoulders brush the narrow stalls as I collect trash and soiled toilet paper and sweep away pubic hair. The cleaning agents suck the moisture from my hands and the skin breaks over my knuckles. I carry clinking bags of waste over my shoulders to the red-brick alleyway, dump them in the bin, and pause to breathe in the cool damp air of Seattle. As instructed, I clean the surrounding area with Clorox water, and it floods the rats out of their dens. They appear from their usual dark corners and step over broken beer glass and bottle caps. I chase at them with a sharp-bristled broom, but they crawl back. I sweep at them repeatedly, each time harder than the next, but they only scurry between my feet. Something touches my ankle and I jump back, kicking off one rat from my foot. I need to step away for a moment. When I gather my courage again, I splash more Clorox water onto the sticky surface and black rodents. My shoes slosh in the pools of dark water. Hunched over, I scoop up the muck one dustpan at a time and dump it into the trash bins. I scrub away at the filth and at the wading rats who seem to taunt me, knowing it will never be clean enough.

I tear off my apron and walk back inside the restaurant. I imagine charging through the kitchen's swinging doors, into Mrs. Kelly's office, and telling her who I really and rightly am. But at the bar I see the soft-spoken, white-haired Mr. Kelly hunched over a beer. "Hello, Mr. Kelly," I say.

I hurry to the bathroom to scrub my hands with soapy, hot water. I wet my face and neck at the sink and for a moment let my head hang over the running faucet. Minutes later, I put on my apron again, and return to my duties in the now-vacant kitchen.

Mrs. Kelly steps out from her office and locks the door behind her. "Prep the food for tomorrow, and lock up when you're finished," she says. I wipe my wet forehead with wet forearm over a pile of dirty dishes and watch the kitchen become eerily still as Mrs. Kelly leaves. She holds her husband's hand, while I chop tomorrow's vegetables.

Later, I rack the last of the dishes, turn off the machines, toss off my splotched apron, shut off all the lights, and walk out the back door, through the alley, and up the hill toward my bus stop.

✦

One morning, when wanting to track the scent of my father inside the familiar layout of a hardware store, I come upon a day laborer by the name of Pablo. He combs the corners of the parking lot for work that often takes him to the city's outskirts. He reminds me of my father. I buy him food. We talk. He's quiet at first. Some days there is no work, he says. He and the other day laborers huddle on the curbside, hiding among the hedges, fiercely watchful of both police and slow-moving vehicles that solicit their services. It is what he knows.

After a while, Pablo tells me the following story:

One day not long ago, Pablo encountered a rusted truck that rolled up next to him. Inside, a gray-haired man in a green hat shouted, "Work? *Tra-ba-jo?*" Pablo nodded in affirmation. The driver reached over and opened the door. Pablo climbed into the passenger side, as he had done with many employers before. Routine.

In Puebla, Mexico, where Pablo is from, most of the townspeople cultivate beans. There is no getting ahead in that town, he says. His aging parents will need caring for soon. He left for the U.S. with plans to earn enough to return home, proudly open his own convenience store, and properly care for his parents. Never would he tell them that he sleeps under bridges at night—living essentially the same hard life as in Mexico, but in English.

Inside the truck were papers, trash, and old cassettes. It smelled of diesel and mold. The driver of the truck mumbled, tobacco under his lip. His hand covered a black bag to his side. His feet brushed against empty beer cans. When Pablo arrived at the worksite in a quiet suburb, he saw a sun-peeled brown house, two rusted junkers among tall grasses, and a black dog pulling at its chains and snarling. Still, Pablo waited eagerly for his assignment.

"See those trees?" the driver said. Young, lush, and about six feet tall. "I want you to uproot them. Here's a shovel. I'll be back at lunchtime with food," he wrapped up and drove off in his rumbling truck. Pablo then hacked around the base of the first tree with the small, rusted shovel thrown at his feet earlier. He figured they would be transplanted and took care not to strike at the major roots. When he came across roots entwined around a large block of stubborn earth, he dug a circle around the tree to loosen its grip without damaging it. He worked fast, and was confident that his strength would not fail him. He piled dirt in a mound and dislodged rocks from the net of wooly roots. When the base of the first tree loosened, he pulled, pushed, and shook it until the tree fell over. The roots crackled like knuckles as the earth released them. He dug around the second tree and did the same. The grooved wooden handle of the shovel gave him splinters, and rubbed his palms until the skin blistered. His hands burned and his arms ached. By tree number three, Pablo's forehead throbbed. His stomach grumbled. The day grew darker, and still there was no sign of his employer.

Late that evening his employer returned and found Pablo sitting on the trunk of one of the uprooted trees, chatting with an elderly neighbor lady. Pablo stood. He had never uprooted a tree before, but he felt positive about his work. His employer approached him, frowning, and said, "You didn't go home yet? You said you'd take the bus home."

"No, señor," Pablo said and waited for further instruction.

There was a pause. The boss spit black chew over the mound of dirt and turned to his truck. "Come. I'll take you back," he said. Pablo waved at the smiling elderly lady. She had reminded him of his mother. She had promised to employ him soon for shoveling snow.

Pablo and the man drove along in the truck. Conifer trees surrounded the road. In a light drizzle, and in the woods, any city lights behind them soon disappeared.

"Cerveza?" the man offered.

"No, gracias," Pablo said. Under a new moon, the hills appeared to grow taller. When the truck turned in the wrong direction, Pablo began to worry. Work had never taken him this far from the city limits.

The passenger door was unlocked. Pablo put his hand on the door handle. "Where are we going?" he asked. His heart raced. His throat tightened. Fear gripped him. The only sound along the dark and winding road was the grumble of the speeding truck. What was he doing with his life? He remembered a question once asked of him by a former employer: "Is life better here or in Mexico?"

It was moments like these, in the truck, or experiencing hunger under bridges, and standing long hours on corners, that made the question difficult to answer. But if asked, he still answers, "Life is better here. By a little."

"Señor?" Pablo tries again.

Without answer, the driver scowled at the wet road.

"Señor, just pay me my money and drop me off here," Pablo said. Then the truck slowed and turned onto a gravel road. Potholes shook the truck's frame. Branches whipped the side of the vehicle. Pablo rolled his window down and wet leaves struck him. Pablo finally opened the door in desperation, put his foot inches over the moving road, and picked a spot among the weeds. "*Dejeme aqui.*"

Pablo jumped.

The truck came to a sliding halt and slowly reversed to where Pablo lay cowering. The driver reached into his back pocket, tossed something into the darkness at Pablo's feet, slammed the passenger door shut, and sped off in reverse down the tight gravel road. The truck's headlights became globes that faded through the dark trees. Pablo rose, took a deep breath, picked up what were seven wet dollars, and limped back along the dark muddy road.

40

Today

These days, Mazat is at work as a psychologist. He does *temazcal*—i.e., sweat and danza once a week with youth and adults with a history of substance abuse. Since first discovering PDJ, Mazat continues to dedicate his life to ceremony, running and traveling all over Latin America to teach and learn from others. "I live for ceremony," he says. He's an avid reader, leads workshops in the mountains, and is a student of poetry and kung fu.

✦

Zyanya Lonewolf is at work with little kids reviving the old ways in her hometown in British Columbia, Canada, by teaching the traditional language of Dakelh at an elementary school and working with other women of her community.

✦

Cheeto works in the Bay Area at a local YMCA. The run is still with him, as well as the memories of all the locals across North America who sacrificed their resources to receive us, offering whatever food and shelter they could. Cheeto never took that lightly and does what he can to pass it forward in his community.

✦

Pacquiao lives in Phoenix, Arizona, managing a local nonprofit and helping bring resources to local Indigenous youth. He still works with PDJ.

✦

Andrec is at home in Fresno, California. When his mother was dying, he took her a bundle of her favorite perennials—sage, soaked in water in a *paño* bandana because the hospital did not allow for burning. That was her favorite smell in the world. His mother breathed it in with Andrec at her side.

After the death of his mother, Andrec gave away his feathers, no longer needing them because, he says, "The strength is inside you. On the run, you just got to shed yourself of all those things. Your will is your true strength."

✦

Chula Pepper is back in San Diego, California, as a happy single mother of one son, Paz. She plans to circle back to the PDJ run in 2020, to run as mother with son.

✦

Tlaloc passed away in a car crash. It killed him and his baby, Megcenetkew—a name that means "the Reflection of the Moon on the Water"—and hospitalized Crow.

The burial, which drew people from all corners of the earth, was a blend of different traditions. Native music and drums played while people lined up behind four shovels and took turns moving earth over Tlaloc and sealing him and his baby to the spirit world. Rival gang members participated peacefully in the ceremony.

✦

Crow is at home today in the wild mountains with her and Tlaloc's twelve-year-old daughter, Malinali, currently fighting against the oil pipeline development threatening their clean water. Still a warrior. With her sister, Crow started a group that fights the ski lodges deforesting their land and bulldozing over homes. They began building houses on wheels that easily relocate, without losing their homes permanently. Malinali ran in PDJ in 2016 and is growing up to be part of the movement with her mother, to carry on the struggle of her people. "We fight," Crow says, "so our children can have a better future."

✦

Ipana is working harder than ever to protect the caribou in Alaska.

✦

Refugio continues to break barriers, still running with the staffs wherever they take him. He was last known to be living in Chiapas.

✦

Trigger is raising a family with Kara in Canada.

✦

Me, I work in Boston, a city of immigrants. When I'm not completing shifts as a security officer at the Boston Athenæum, one of the oldest independent libraries in the country, I wander.

On one such walk in the city, I come upon a faint Pepsi sign that hangs from rusted hinges on the side of an old brick building. At first glance it looks abandoned and, like a mesmerized moth to a lamp, I approach this small outpost of the past—still a believer that structures like these hold a certain wisdom. I decipher its dim lettering—bowling center—like I do the code of the streets: walk like you know where you're going. I step into the pale light of a single bulb shining over the entrance where a chair is stationed outside. Inside, I hear the roar of men. I take a deep breath and push through two pairs of swinging doors, into thick, mildewed air. The smell of the past.

Three older men of seeming Italian and Irish descent, fit, are leaned over a counter, engaged in some dispute. They don track jackets, tattoos, and towels over shoulders. Between them: a stack of money and scratched lotto tickets. Sports stream from a nearby television and tacked to the faux-wood walls is an American flag and a Keno Lottery banner.

"Lemme tell you somethin'—" one man in a Boston accent exclaims to another in a corroded smoker's voice. The grain of a shouter. Jewelry-adorned hands slam onto the counter in heated gesture.

They turn to me, straight-faced.

I feel like I should speak carefully but nothing comes to mind. "I'm looking for a place to—" They glance questioningly at one another. "A place to buy a drink, maybe do some work?" I'm nervous. It's clear that I'm not from around here. I tell them that I'm looking for a home away from home, a place to moor myself among good and interesting people.

They laugh.

"Well, you've come to the right place," they tell me. The ice thaws. "All sorts of characters here."

For hours I watch these men from the sidelines—how they clasp candlepin balls to their chests as if in prayer and rub them for good luck like crystal balls. I can't help but feel like I've been missing out on something special in my own life. The men's eyes watch over the wooden floors as if reading an old roadmap to when they were younger. For me, to when I was nineteen years old, restless, and on the run with Indigenous people. In many ways, still on the run.

Before I part ways with everyone, I think about how here human connection thrives, just like it did on the run with Peace and Dignity Journeys. Where people on the community level are taking back their lives. Where people are prioritized and flaws are part of the human narrative.

"Come back and see us," they say.

✦

These days, my mother lives alone, content among a swarm of wasps in her backyard, in a small rental in west Yakima that she fills with picture frames of her old life when we were all kids and still in need of her. A house finely decorated the way she always wanted. Not a moving box in sight. She turns off the television—a Spanish religious channel, and as always, she receives us with food.

When I visit her, she gives me a tour of the kitchen, her cabinets, and refrigerator. Proud. "Look, all the best foods," she says. "And my car," she says, opening the garage door connected to the side of the house, "it's all paid off finally."

"I'm very proud of you, Amá," I tell her.

We sit and eat warm tortillas on the back patio, beneath the bees, overlooking the lawn and the remnants of a burned-down house. She walks onto the lawn and spikes the water sprinkler into a new area before finally seating herself next to me. She touches my arm.

"Want me to call someone about the bees?" I ask her.

"No. They're harmless. They don't do anything," she says. They're her company, her protection.

"Tomorrow, very early, I'm taking Dad fishing," I say.

"You're still fishing, mijo?" She looks off into the distance. "I've prepared the bed for you. It's there whenever you need it."

✦

My father continues to work in construction. For our fishing trip, I leave my mother's house at an hour when the world is still sleeping, save the laborers, construction workers, and everyone else whose job it is to wake before sunrise. I walk a couple miles through crisp air to where my dad lives, fishing pole slung over my shoulder in its case. The air has a special smell at this hour, rewarding for only those who can wake up early enough to experience it. It's the smell of coffee that first hits me when I meet my dad hunched over the sink in the kitchen. A smell that woke me so many times as a boy back when he worked in the orchards. The living room is dark.

"I have pan dulce," he tells me while walking to his truck. He makes room for me in his truck—still his mobile office. Letters, papers, his carpentry tools and other equipment. I miss the clutter. He places a five-gallon bucket of tools at the feet of the passenger seat, and I squeeze in. Dust kicks up from the seat, and I am once again enveloped in my father's smell. Happiness. I am like a kid again en route to the orchard. He starts the old truck and we drive into the blue light where the sun slowly rises, watching these old lands again, with renewed longing, through a cracked and bug-plastered windshield. He still keeps pennies in the ashtray, many pairs of sunglasses, camouflage trucker hats, and ear plugs.

"Can I wear these?" I put on a pair of his shades and his hat, look into the side-view mirror—proud to wear the look of a father I'm no longer ashamed of.

He drives me to Wapato to a lake accessible via a tight tunnel under a bridge. Here, I teach him to fly fish.

He retreats to a nearby tree and squats. "I'll watch you." I glance at his figure on my back cast. It's been many years since I've seen him squatted like that, in that look, under a tree next to a large canteen of water. For years the trees were this family's sanctuary. A family that congregated under apple trees with their children for lunch, took respite, and played music to mitigate long days.

"Come. You try now." He comes and I give him the rod.

"Hold it this way." I teach him about the fly, the cast, and loading the rod. In minutes he catches a fish and he runs after it like a kid, holding the fish in his hand before releasing it.

The sun keeps pace with us.

"I know a better place," he says after about an hour. "Get your things," and we drive from place to place as if to catch up on the years we missed together.

We cast the river on Canyon Road, then a lake more like a watering hole for cattle, before finally settling on little Tjossem Pond. Again and again we shout, "Got another one!" I can't remember the last time we caught so many fish. The day passes too quickly and the hour arrives when I have to leave again.

"Bus gets here in a couple hours," I remind him. "Mom's taking me to the station."

I'm still often conflicted about the things I want and the things I need. I want to be in Washington State again, a place of soul, among family, nesting and healing on a land that has given me so much spirit. But what I need is to carry this spirit forward, into new lands, making decisions based on the future. To continue to run toward the best version of myself, even if it pains me to wander from a place I will always call home. I fool myself into getting onto a Greyhound bus to Seattle to board a flight back to Boston. No one knows me there. I can try on new faces, pursue new opportunities. Boston.

✦

I return to my apartment in Boston to ready myself for work the next day where I will put on a suit and tie and ready myself for a shift as a security officer at the Boston Athenæum.

I enter the employee entrance of the museum through the security corridor and hang up my wet coat from rain. I set the morning's newspapers onto a small table and access my locker where I surrender my wallet and collect my red notebook, earpiece, and two-way radio—radio number five. I clip it and an ID badge to my belt. I connect my earpiece and clock in. When all is 10-4, I review the CCTV camera footage and watch staff settle into their work spaces on chairs and desks, to be absorbed in the business of books.

I adjust my tie, unlock the front doors, and take post at the vestibule. I am a pillar among mainly white spaces, accompanied by the decapitated head of Zeus erect above an Athena statue, as well as a large painting of the flaying of Marsyas—the violent depiction of a man who's skinned alive at the hands of Apollo. Members' coats are stacked like shadowy remnants of their owners near the reading room that houses the marble statue of a paraplegic Greek man. Art is violent.

Here, I contend not only with the mental fatigue of museum silence, but the nervous reality that has haunted and pestered me all of my life: that I will always be working-class.

The clacking dress shoes over marble floors remind me that I am surrounded by people who know where they're going in life. In these small spaces, even in the most trivial of conversations, I pretend that I matter, that people value my insight into random matters of life, literature, and local events.

Every hour on the hour, I complete a tour of the building, starting from level five down to the basement, lower levels, and boiler room, securing all areas, and walking in the many shadows of prominent white men preserved as busts. To pass the time, I peruse the pages of the many oversize dictionaries around the library. I read the words. *Retrolenticular*: "that which is situated behind the lens of the eye." It snags my attention. The ability to look beyond that which is in front of you, I wonder, trying to strip meaning from the curious word. To see behind the image of things. For what they really are. I step back into the shadow of my post, cross my arms, and sink back into what may or may not be my true form, where I will remain watched by Zeus, Athena, tortured by the flaying of a man named Marsyas, and cameras.

At closing time, I do a thorough sweep of the building, clear and secure all areas of ghosts, shutting off all lights and navigating a sea of dark history with a flashlight, never forgetting the shelf of brittle books aged like tobacco leaves: ledgers of the slave trade. I surrender my two-way radio and sever myself from this world for the night. I wrap up any paperwork, collect my belongings, and close the back entrance's door behind me. I walk to the train station at Boston Common.

On the train, I hold my bag between my arms, staring out at the dark underground of the city, while biting into my thumbnail. What's left of it, that is. The T map splits over the doors like a tributary of veins, detailing the many Boston stops. My stop is at the end of the line. I dig and dig into my nail until it bleeds. A construction man, weighed down by heavy tool bags and boots, moves into the train and plops into a corner. There are sounds of him rubbing his fingers over his unshaven face. Three Latina women laugh without restraint over a video on their phone. They are people who know how to enjoy the small things in life. The train resurfaces near Northeastern University where throngs of students crosshatch the night streets. It rains. We pass a fire station where a wet American flag slaps against its pole like a slab of meat.

At home in my apartment, I can never tear it off fast enough—my tie, suit, button-up shirt, dress shoes that change meaning once inside my apartment. Like shedding snake skin.

Tomorrow is another run.

Acknowledgments

For cracking open my spirit and giving me religion, i.e., running: my friends at Peace and Dignity Journeys 2004.

For tirelessly championing this story throughout the literary world: Rebecca Gradinger at Fletcher and Company.

For her advocacy, kind edits, and for giving me restraint when I wanted to yell on the page: Megha Majumdar at Catapult.

For her loving mentorship and for steering me through the world of memoir: Theo Nestor.

For teaching me all there is to know about fiction: Scott T. Driscoll.

For reeling me in from the slush pile: Christy Fletcher at Fletcher and Company.

For their enthusiasm: Hilary Zaits Michael and Carolina Beltran at William Morris Endeavor.

For their vital support: the staff at Catapult, Fletcher and Company, and Counterpoint Press.

For their friendship: Jesus Castañeda Flores, Rigo, Matt Magee, Pedro Meza, Rachel Dexter.

For the kind invitation: New England Independent Booksellers Association, Mountains & Plains Independent Booksellers Association, Pacific Northwest Booksellers Association.

For the structures that housed my restless spirit: A.C. Davis High School, Whitman College, Princeton University, American University, and Emerson College.

For the landscapes that molded me: Yakima, Washington, the Greenway trail along the Yakima and Naches rivers, and Bob and Claudette's apple orchard (may they rest in peace).

© Mia Concordia

NOÉ ÁLVAREZ was born to Mexican immigrant parents and raised working-class in Yakima, Washington. He holds degrees in philosophy and creative writing from Whitman College and Emerson College, respectively. He studied conflict analysis, peacemaking, and conflict resolution at American University and in Northern Ireland, received a fellowship at Princeton University's Woodrow Wilson School, and researched U.S. drug policy, military aid, and human rights issues in Colombia's Putumayo jungles. He lives in Boston, where, until recently, he worked as a security officer at one of the nation's oldest libraries, the Boston Athenæum.